Pra

La___r_te

1994

Hayit Publishing

Using this Book

Books in the series *Practical Travel* offer a wealth of practical information. You will find the most important tips for your travels conveniently arraged in alphabetical order. Cross- references aid in orientation so that even entries which are not covered in depth, for instance "Holiday Apartments", lead you to the appropriate entry, in this case "Accommodation".

Also, thematically altered entries are also cross-referenced. For example under the heading "Banks", there appears the reference "Money", or under the heading "Natural Protection" appears the reference "Animals and Wildlife." With travel guides from the series *Practical Travel* the information is already available before you depart on your trip. Thus, you are already familiar with necessary travel documents and maps, even customs regulations. Travel within the country is made easier through comprehensive presentation of public transportation, car rentals in addition to the practical tips ranging from medical assistance to newspapers available in the country.

The descriptions of cities are arranged alphabetically as well and include the most important facts about the particular city, its history and a summary of significant sights. In addition, these entries include a wealth of practical tips – from shopping, restaurants and accommodation to important local addresses. Background information does not come up short either. You will find interesting information about the people and their culture as well as the regional geography, history and current political and economic situation.

As a particular service to our readers, *Practical Travel* includes prices in pounds sterling and dollars so that they might gain a more accurate impression of prices even in countries with high rates of inflation.

Hayit

Travel Guides

Practical travel guides from **Hayit Publishing** can be found at your local bookseller. If you'd like more information we'd be happy to send you our catalogue with all of Hayit's titles currently available.

REQUEST FORM

☐ **Yes**, please send me your current catalogue with all **Hayit Publishing** titles free of charge and with no obligation.

Name:

Street Address:

City/Town:

Postal Code:

Telephone:

Fax:

POST CARD

Hayit Publishing
c/o Amalgamated
Book Services Ltd.
Royal Star Arcade, Suite 1
High Street
Maidstone ME 14 1JL
Great Britain

Current practical information is essential for a quality travel guide. Although every effort was made during our research to keep this guide up to date, prices and other information can change rapidly — sometimes within weeks. For this reason, we would be grateful for any comments, suggestions or information you might have concerning Lanzarote.
Hayit Publishing, c/o Amalgamated Book Services Ltd., Suite 1, Royal Star Arcade, High Street, Maidstone Kent ME14 1JL.

1st Edition 1994
ISBN: 1 874251 16 9

Author: Peter Kensok
Editoral Assistant: Shireen Esmail
Translation, Adaption, Revision: Scott Reznik
Assistant Editor (English version): Sabarah Hanif
Typesetting: Hayit Publishing
Print: Druckhaus Cramer, Greven/Germany
Photography: Renate Tarrach
Maps: Ralf Tito

2.3/Rs//Rs

Lanzarote —
the bizarre fascination of a volcanic island

Lanzarote is not only popular as a holiday destination in the Atlantic throughout the year but holds geological and cultural fascination as well. Eruptions during the 18th century blanketed over one-fourth of the island's surface with a layer of lava and ash, leaving behind a bizarre lunar landscape and caverns. Two of these caverns are among Lanzarote's main attractions: Cueva de los Verdes and Jameos del Agua. The latter is a product of nature in conjunction with the artistic vision of the island's most famous resident, César Manrique.

Craters on Lanzarote are not all volcanic in origin; some of these are the result of ingenious agricultural methods employed on the island to coax grapevines out of this stingy soil. The result is not only excellent wines but a cultivated landscape unique throughout the world.

Extensive opuntia cactus fields add splotches of colour to the dark profile of this island and are simultaneously the habitat of cochineal lice — a species which produces a pigment used in cosmetics.

Still untouched in many regions, Lanzarote has a lot to offer hikers. And one just may need sturdy hiking boots to reach some of the more secluded beaches.

Whether experiencing Lanzarote's untamed nature or challenging the waves on a surfboard, this island is the perfect combination of a sunny beach holiday, culture and rugged beauty.

Contents

Registry of Places

General Information

Accommodation

Spain is well organised in terms of tourism – this is especially true regarding accommodation. The tourist information offices (→*Tourist Information*) will send lists of hotels, campsites and apartments in various regions upon request. When sent directly from the tourist information offices, these lists are usually up-to-date including the most current prices.

Information on the Canary Islands may not be the most current, and one can be surprised by an enormous price increase. This, however, is a result of the high rate of inflation. The actual price per night is posted at every officially recognised accommodation.

Whether private accommodation or a hotel, the premises are inspected and the result is posted next to or above the main entrance. The following are the various categories of accommodation available in Spain:

AT = Apartamentos. Apartments are fully furnished with one or two bedrooms, a shower or bath, and usually a kitchenette or even a living room. This category is subdivided according to the number of keys:

One key – here, there is usually hot water or a shower and a lift in buildings with more than four floors

Two keys – there is a house telephone at the reception, hot water on every floor, heating and lifts in buildings with more than three floors.

Three keys – heating, hot water, lifts in buildings with more than three floors, reception area, telephone calls can be connected to each apartment.

Four keys – luxury category. Air conditioning, lifts in buildings with more than two floors, heating, hot water during the entire day, telephone.

CH = Casa Huespedes. Very simple accommodation.

CV = Club de Vacaciones. This type of accommodation is increasing in popularity: the so called "time sharing", whereby members buy a share of the accommodation for a given number of weeks during a year. This type of accommodation is only available to club members.

F = Fonda. This is the least expensive type of accommodation for those who do not have high expectations in terms of comfort.

H = Hotels and Guest Houses are subdivided into categories depending on the number of stars (*):

* Heating, lift in buildings with over four floors, shower or sink in every fourth room, a bath shared by at most seven rooms, telephone on each floor, laundry service possible.

** Lift in buildings with more than three floors, reception area, bar, private bath in every eighth room, shower, sink toilet available in every second room. Telephone in every room.

*** Heating, lift, reception area, bar, complete bath in every second room, telephone in every room.

**** Air conditioning in every room and bedroom, heating, lift, at least two reception areas, bar, equipped with a parking garage in cities, the majority of rooms include a private bath, in others, usually a toilet and sink, telephone in every room.

***** Air conditioning in every room, central heating, at least two lifts, several reception areas, laundry service possible, telephone in every room, bar, parking garage, salon on the premises.

HR = Hotel Residencia. A hotel which does not offer full board.

HS = Hostal. Guest house which almost meets the standards of a hotel but is offered at a more reasonable price.

HSR = Hostal-Residencia. Guest house which does not serve lunch or dinner.

P = Pension. Usually includes a restaurant, but one does not need to purchase full board.

For accommodation – whether hotel, apartment in the lower categories – one must plan on spending £7 ($12. 50) to £14 ($25) per day.

The only two Canarian youth hostels are on Gran Canaria.

Three campsites can only be found on the island of Gran Canaria and Tenerife has two (→*Camping*).

For further information on accommodation (→*individual entries*).

Accommodation on Lanzarote

In regard to accommodation, Lanzarote is well equipped especially in the four tourist centres of Arrecife, Playa Blanca, Puerto del Carmen and Costa Teguise. For the other towns, hotels, guest houses and holiday apartments are listed under the individual entries in this guide.

Airport

The "Guasimeta" Airport – only 7 kilometres (4¼ miles) south of Arrecife – began its evolution as a military airport in 1940. The first commercial flight to fly from Las Palmas (Gran Canaria) to Arrecife was a DC 3 which landed at Guasimeta Airport in 1950. One year later, officials registered 2,000 guests who arrived on Lanzarote by air. Beginning in 1971, over 300,000 air passengers arrived at Guasimeta annually; of them, 35,000 were visitors from foreign countries. Today, the airport can by no means accommodate the floods of holiday visitors. The appeals to expand the terminal in the interest of efficiency meanwhile become louder: every Thursday alone, 110 flights must be handled, which translates to almost six every hour around the clock. Airport personnel is already being increased solely to handle baggage.

Thursday at 2 in the afternoon is the absolute "rush hour", with over 1,200 passengers arriving and departing. Twenty four tons of luggage must be checked and loaded onto the planes. To ensure that all of the passengers can even be processed, the domestic flights terminal must be opened to international passengers; otherwise, the airport would offer only two square metres (22 square feet per passenger). International regulations 10 square metres (108 square feet). The way the situation has been solved at present, each passenger has 12 square metres (130 square feet) at his or her disposal while waiting for departure.

As reported by José Infante (director of the airport since 1984) to the islands newspaper "Lancelot", the actual requirements for Lanzarote are presently being investigated. Plans exist to expand Lanzarote's airport by 1995.

Information: Tel: 81 14 50
Police: Tel: 81 11 54 and 81 36 36

Animals and Wildlife

There are 30 to 40 thousand cattle living on the Canary Islands, usually kept in stables and fed banana plants. Then, there are also sheep and, in addition to some dromedaries and camels, there are only goats, goats and more goats. The latter are not a blessing for this island with sparse vegetation in some regions because they eat plants and shrubs down to the roots – and this is true for just about any plant. The dromedaries and camels limit their diet to the thorny bushes and halophyte shrubs.

The rabbits also present a threat; however, they are also threatened: on the Canary Islands, around 15,000 hunting licences are granted annually. For every square kilometre there are at least four hunters.

There are no snakes or scorpions on the island, but there are lizards (Lacerta simonyi), especially geckos. The largest lizards (Lacerta simonyi) on Gran Canaria can grow up to 80 centimetres (27 inches) in length. A special species of reptile are the skinks which are often mistaken for snakes because of their slender bodies and the fact that they are sometimes legless. These are harmless and interesting to watch. Lizards, doves, ravens, thrushes and ants make themselves ecologically useful, spreading the seeds of tomatoes and grapes as well as laurel and dragon trees.

Dogs, cats and donkeys are among the most common domestic animals on the Canary Islands. The Canary bird can also be counted among these. The talkative species was in fact named after these islands.

Animals and Wildlife on Lanzarote

Lanzarote is not far from Africa and it is exactly for this reason that Lanzarote's fauna is African – at least when the picture of the dromedaries and camels comes to mind, which can be ridden on portions of the island as well as the neighbouring island of Graciosa. Earlier, these animals were predominantly used in agriculture. Today, their main function lies elsewhere. The business in tourism has definitely become more attractive than using these animals to draw a plough, a job where a tractor could easily be substituted. Numerous camels and dromedaries can be found in →*Uga* and → *Yaiza*. From these towns, the animals are used for excursions to the Montañas del Fuego.

Live horsepower: donkeys belong to the everyday in the villages on Lanzarote

Arrecife

The capital of Lanzarote, Arrecife, is around 7 kilometres (4¼ miles) from the airport and offers two sandy beaches. This city has a population of 29,500 not counting the tourists. The holiday town of →*Puerto del Carmen* lies 15 kilometres (9½ miles) from Arrecife and it is around 40 kilometres (25 miles) to →*Playa Blanca.* Arrecife is a somewhat atypical city for the Canary Islands: instead of the characteristic colourful Canarian balconies, the buildings have wooden shutters and sliding doors. During low tide, rock reefs can be seen protruding from the water, which inspired the name Arrecife. The narrow alleyways leading through the old city district and the marketplace are only two attractions which this city has to offer.

Without a doubt, Arrecife is the economic and touristic focal point on the island of Lanzarote, especially due to its nearby harbour. Freight is handled here and tourists also arrive and depart at this harbour.

The main roads on the island all converge in Arrecife and the city is also the seat of the political bodies and administration. Still, Arrecife is only in second place behind the population centres of →*Tias* with →*Puerto del Carmen* both in terms of tourism as well as growth in population. There is only limited money to be made in Arrecife; the city has developed over time and does not allow for the construction as is taking place in the southern portions of the island where the tourists are.

The fishing harbour of Naos, earlier one of the main sources of income, has long since lost its former significance for the city. Young people also demonstrate against the insular government and the unions who plan on striking trainee positions in fishing and dissolving training centres. The question remains how long there will still be sardine and tuna canneries which have provided many residents of Arrecife with an income.

The city is simultaneously beautiful and ugly. There are districts which are very poor and wealthy hoteliers. The limited portion of the tourists who do stay in Arrecife are the source of prosperity for the hotels lining the Avenida Mancomunidad. The prices are correspondingly high. On the other hand, the tourism boom has fostered the development of four competing centres on the island: Arrecife, →*Costa Teguise,* →*Puerto del Carmen* and →*Playa Blanca.* If one includes →*La Caleta* and *Playa de Famara,* then it is five.

This means, for example in the case of renting a car, that a buyer's market prevails and customers must be attracted with the best possible prices.

→*Car Rental* and →*Arrecife / Practical Information* below.

Arrecife / **Sights**

The landmark of the city is without a doubt the Gran Hotel high-rise at the end of Avenida Mancomunidad at the beginning of the Playa del Reducto beach. The famous artist →*César Manrique* takes a distant stance from this four-star hotel: he was in America at the time that this hotel was built and claims that he is innocent of this architectural faux pas. The hotel towers above the beach, secluded from the other buildings in the city centre and is visible from quite a distance, similar to a lighthouse.

The Avenida Mancomunidad is the entertainment strip in Arrecife. Hotels and bars line this avenue and during the evening the coastal promenade of Generalisimo Franco is full of people.

In the centre of the city across from the Gran Hotel (the only high-rise on Lanzarote which lives up to the term) is the culture centre "El Almacen", Calle José Bethancourt 26-36, Tel: 81 24 16 and 81 24 17. Here, one can enjoy a meal or a beverage or visit the "El Aljibe" Gallery. The culture centre is open from 6 to 9 pm.

Near the harbour only a little way from the "San José" fortress is the Castillo de San Gabriele. It is situated on an island across from the centre of Arrecife. The Venetian architect Leonardo Torriani built this structure in 1590. The fortress as well as the Castillo were intended to protect the city from pirate attacks. Ten cannons – now replaced with replicas – seem to have sufficed at that time. "San Gabriele" is connected to the city by a drawbridge called "Puente de las Bolas" (bridge of cannonballs) by the local residents.

This fortress is presently being remodelled as an archaeological museum. The exhibitions are already open to the public: on display are documents relating to the cultural history of Lanzarote. Admission costs around 50¢ (30p). The museum is open Monday to Friday from 8 am to 1 pm. There is also a patrolled parking area across from the museum. No entrance fee is charged for the museum of contemporary art.

The "Castillo San José" is situated between the Mole Los Marmoles and the port of Naos. It was built under the orders of King Carlos III and was needed to ward off attacks by Moorish and European pirates on the city and the neighbouring port of Naos. To protect it from the rigours of time, through which the building was slowly deteriorating, César Manrique built a museum inside it which concentrates on contemporary art by both Spanish and foreign artists. There is a stylish yet homey restaurant in the cellar of this building. The museum as well as the restaurant are open from 11am to 9 pm.

The Playa del Reducto beach near the Castillo San Gabriele is well-maintained; unfortunately, seaweed does washed up on the beach, making

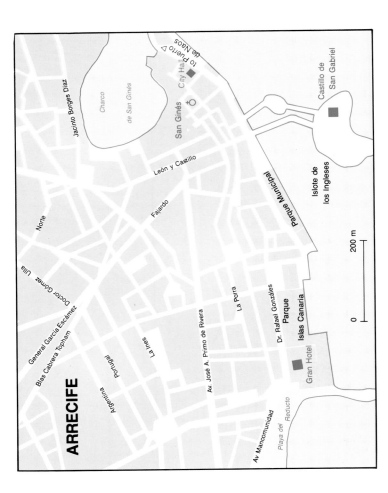

sunbathing or swimming less attractive on this stretch of beach. The next attractive beach is that of →*Playa Honda*. Arrecife is, therefore, less widely known and less popular for its beaches than for its shopping. The catchword here is "Calle León y Castillo". This is simultaneously the banking quarter and the main shopping street.

If coming from the "Puente de las Bolas" passing the "San Gabriele" fortress, and onto Calle León y Castillo, the insular administration building can be seen on the right-hand side. Continuing down the street on the right is a just as modern but unfortunately almost deserted shopping centre with various shops and restaurants. Taking a look inside doesn't cost anything but time and it may even be possible to find this or that souvenir at a better price than in Puerto del Carmen. In addition, there are public toilets here.

There is one department store after the other as well as the numerous banks on León y Castillo. It is quite an experience to take a stroll down this street among the local residents of Arrecife. The traditional market, the Mercado on Calle Libre not far from the San Gines Church and the religious book store has meanwhile even become a destination offered by tour organisers on the island.

The San Gines Church was renovated in 1988. Supports were added to the roof and the timeworn interior was given new lustre. This church, named after the patron saint of Lanzarote, was intended as a place of piety and worship.

Arrecife / **Practical Information**

Accommodation

"Arrecife Gran Hotel" (***), Avenida Mancomunidad, Tel: 81 12 50. 150 rooms priced from £55 ($94).

Hotel/Residencia "Lanzelot Playa" (***), Avenida Mancomunidad, Tel: 81 14 00. 123 rooms priced from £26 ($44).

Hotel/Residencia "Miramar" (***), Coll 2, Tel: 81 04 38. 90 rooms priced from £30 ($50).

Hotel/Residencia "San Gines", Molino 9, Tel: 81 23 51. 28 rooms priced from £18 ($32).

Hotel/Residencia "Cardona" (***), 18 de Julio, Tel: 81 10 08. 62 rooms with doubles priced from £18 ($32).

Hotel/Residencia "Alepsa" (*), Calle León y Castillo 52, Tel: 81 17 56. 13 rooms with doubles priced from £15 ($25).

Hostal "España", Gran Canaria 4, Tel: 81 11 90. 26 rooms priced from £11 ($19).

Hotel/Residencia "Tisalaya", Perez Galdos 12, Tel: 81 15 85. 9 rooms priced from £15 ($25).

"Castillo del Papagayo" Apartment House (three keys), Charco de Palo. 7 apartments priced from £30 ($50).

"Arrecife Playa" Apartment House (two keys), Avenida Mancomunidad 4, Tel: 81 03 00. Apartments priced from £22 to £33 ($38 to $57).

"Islamar" Apartment House (two keys), Avenida Rafael Gonzales 15, Tel: 81 15 00. 17 apartments priced from £26 ($44).

"Rubicon" Apartment House (two keys), Avenida Mancomunidad 8, Tel: 81 12 48. 6 apartments priced from £26 ($44).

Bus Terminal

The bus terminal is located across from the "El Reducto Menson" Restaurant which can be recognised by its blue windows (Avenida Fred Olsen, near the Gran Hotel). A bus ticket to Playa Blanca (40 kilometres/25 miles) via Tias, Puerto del Carmen, Uga, Yaiza and Las Breñas) costs around £1.15 ($2).

Car Rental

Autos San José, Avenida Rafael Gonzales Negrin 6, Tel: 81 36 08.

Autos Riverol, Avenida Mancomunidad 24, Tel: 81 01 50 and 81 01 54. Central office in Tias.

Autos Bermudez, Avenida Mancomunidad, in the Gran Hotel annex, Tel: 81 08 34.

Autos Cabrera Medina, Calle Cuba 3, Tel: 81 04 83 and 81 18 76; and Negrin 8, Tel: 91 09 49.

Viajes Timanfaya, Avenida General Franco 6, Tel: 81 58 00, 81 58 04 and 81 58 08.

Autos Morales, Centro Comercial Arrecife, Avenida Mancomunidad, Tel: 81 41 25. One should also compare prices and the rental cars available in the Luis Morote 26 office, Tel: 81 30 23.

Currency Exchange

Banco de Bilbao, León y Castillo 7, Tel: 81 07 00, 81 07 04 and 81 03 97.

Banco Central, León y Castillo 16, Tel: 81 04 50 and 81 17 51.

Banco Exterior de España, Calvo Sotelo 8, Tel: 81 27 00 and 81 27 04.

Banco Español de Credito, León y Castillo 12, Tel: 81 11 66 and 81 11 70.

Banco Hispano Americano, León y Castillo 17, Tel: 81 11 50.

Banco de las Islas Canarias, Plaza Constitución 7, Tel: 81 41 04 and 81 41 00.

Banco de Santander, Alferez Cabrera Tavio 7, Tel: 81 28 00 and 81 26 16.
Banco de Viscaya, León y Castillo 26, Tel: 81 40 08 and 81 40 12.
Caja Insular de Ahorros, León y Castillo 2, Tel: 81 07 58, 81 10 61 and 81 19 12.
Caja Insular de Ahorros, Calle Mexico, Tel: 81 43 62 and 81 43 63.
Caja Insular de Ahorros, Avenida Hernandez Pacheco (Sta. Coloma), Tel: 81 00 59.

Entertainment

The El Almacen Cultural Centre, the Gran Hotel's bar and the terraces on Avenida Mancomunidad are the focal points for Lanzarote's night life. A basement discotheque is often recommenced and this disco is called "Snipe" on Avenida Mancomunidad. However, the music is very loud and the atmosphere, less communicative.

Arrecife is not a hot-spot for disco-goers. Those looking to dance the night away are better off in the discos in →_Puerto del Carmen._

Medical Care

Doctor Marin, Avenida Fred Olsen, Tel: 81 11 38 and 81 11 86.
Hospital Insular, Juan de Quesada 37, Tel: 81 05 00.

Pharmacies

Alfonso Valls Diaz, Calle García Escámez 1, Tel: 81 15 30.
Consuelo Paez, Calle Mexico 70, Tel: 81 25 66.
Juan Armaz Cancio, Calle Eugenio Rijo 11, Tel: 81 07 42.
José Tenorio de Paiz, Calle Pedro Barba 4, Tel: 81 01 26.
Manuel Medina Voltes, Calle Perez Galdos 87, Tel: 81 17 20 and 81 05 60.
Pedro Medina Armas, Fajardo 18, Tel: 81 10 68.
Rogelio Tenorio de Paiz, León y Castillo 43, Tel: 81 10 72.
Viuda de Matallana, León y Castillo 13, Tel: 81 10 93.

Restaurants

"El Reducto Meson" Restaurant, Avenida Fred Olsen 1, Tel: 81 63 89. Across from the Playa del Reducto, this restaurant can be recognised by its blue windows. Prices fit in with the location near the Gran Hotel. Café solo: 55p (95¢).

"Café de Paris", Avenida Mancomunidad, Tel: 81 49 16. The food is good, but for the small portions served it is extremely overpriced. The bread served with a meal costs 55p (95¢); a small broiled fish (enough for a snack) costs £3.30 ($5.65).

Despite this, Café de Paris is one of the nicest restaurants on Arrecife's liveliest street. One can watch the activity from the terrace here for hours on end, especially during midday.

The "Martin" Bar-Restaurante at Plaza de la Constitución 12, directly behind the post office building, is recommended: a complete meal costs between £2.75 and £7.30 ($9.50 and $12.50). This restaurant also serves typically Canarian cuisine. Lanzarote does not have its own distinct cuisine but there are dishes on the menus which can be considered Canarian. Especially the chick-pea soup made with potatoes, paprika and garlic falls under the heading "simple, hearty and delicious".

Fish is served in "Marisquería Abdon" (Calle Canalejas 51, Tel: 81 45 58) for very reasonable prices. This restaurant lives up to its name and has specialised in fish dishes. The fish soups are a matter of personal taste and, as many fish soups served on the Canary Islands, they are rather salty. The soups are priced around £2.20 ($3.75).

Across from the Red Cross Centre on the promenade is a spaghetti restaurant which attracts not only pasta lovers for lunch and dinner. Ice cream and various

Arrecife: the commercial and touristic hub of Lanzarote

pizza creations are served here as well. The view of the promenade and the Generalisimo Franco street offer entertainment in addition to the generous portions served.

Important Addresses

Tourist Information: Parque Municipal, Tel: 81 18 60.
Post and Telegram Office: Avenida del Generalisimo Franco 8, Tel: 81 19 17 and 81 02 41.
City Hall: Vargas 6, Tel: 81 02 93 and 81 13 17.
Iberia Airlines: Avenida del Generalisimo Franco 10, Tel: 81 03 50.
Trasmediterranea: José Antonio, Tel: 81 10 90.
Central Taxi Switchboard: 81 02 83, 81 09 18, 81 07 69, 81 16 80 and 81 17 72.
Police: Apolo 3, Tel: 81 09 46 and 81 11 00; Vargas 6, Tel: 81 13 17.
Patrolled Parking Area: on Castillo San Gabriel, 15p (25¢).

It offered protection from uninvited guests: the drawbridge at the Castillo de San Gabriel in Arrecife

Arrieta

The village of Arrieta is accessible by taking the GC 700 road from Arrecife and turning right toward Cueva de los Verdes and Jameos del Agua when the road curves in Tahiche. Arrieta is 24 kilometres (15 miles) from the island's capital. A few years ago, Arrieta was first and foremost a fishing village. Today, the attractions of the neighbouring beach →*Playa de la Garita* have been recognised and is being developed to attract the town's share of tourists. On the town's main road are a number of restaurants, a souvenir shop and also private accommodation.

Accommodation: The "Ancla" Restaurant on Calle la Marina, rents out apartments starting at £14 ($23). (Category: one key).

Restaurants: There are 5 restaurants on the La Marina road that specialise in fish dishes; "Amanecer", "Ancia", "La Nasa", "Los Pescaditos" and "Miguel". If one would rather have something other than fish, these restaurants do also offer alternatives.

Automobile Clubs

Real Automóbile Club de España (RACE), Madrid 3, Jose Abascal 10, Tel: (91) 4 47 32 00. RACE has branch offices in:

Santa Cruz de Tenerife, Tenerife, Mendez Nuñez 28 and Avenida Anaga; Tel: 27 00 70.

Las Palmas de Gran Canaria, Gran Canaria, Galo Ponte 8.

The Touring Club de España can be contacted through the address: Santa Cruz de Tenerife, Garcia Morato 14; Tel: 27 16 69.

Bargaining

Bargaining at the marketplaces on the Canary Islands is not customary. Those who do not accept these prices should purchase groceries in the supermarkets, in which the products are excellent. It is only worthwhile to try to bargain with the prices in the tourist centres when peddlers or other salespeople demand an exorbitant price for their sunglasses for example. If a price is marked, then the decision is quite simple: to buy, or not to buy.

Beaches

A word regarding the term "Playa": maps of Lanzarote indicate playas all around the island as is the case with the other Canary Islands as well. The word "Playa" is neither an indicator if a beach is suitable for swimming or if a towel has to be spread on gravel, volcanic stones, black or white sand. All it says, in fact, is that water and land meet at this point – and this is the case around any island. In any case, Lanzarote does have quite a few beaches to suit any taste:

Costa Teguise northeast of Arrecife is a holiday centre which was built during the past few years. There is a beach with light fine sand in front of the Las Salinas Hotel.

Playa Blanca is the name of the beach town on the southern end of the island. Even the harbour is suited to swimming. It lies protected behind a mole and even though the fishing boats and the "Alimsur" ferry always stir up some silt, this sandy beach is still not dirty. The famous **Papagayo** beaches lie somewhat outside of Playa Blanca, wrapped around the southern tip of the Punta de Papgayo. There are several bays with light sand or gravel where it is still possible to swim in relative seclusion.

There is a second Playa Blanca near →*Puerto del Carmen*. Adjacent to the northeast of this beach are the sandy beaches of **Playa de los Pocillos** and **Matagorda**. Surfers will feel right at home in this area south of Arrecife. The perfect weather for windsurfers can be found here as well as almost everywhere along Lanzarote's coastline and this throughout the entire year. The optimal beach for more experienced windsurfers are the beaches near →*La Isleta* west of Costa Blanca in Lanzarote's northern regions.

The Atlantic influence is prominent here and the winds are more untamed. On **Playa Famara** near →*La Caleta,* one will find the surf and wind conditions like those on a North Sea island. The fact that an experienced captain ran aground on a reef near La Caleta, breaking his ship in two should definitely serve as a warning to even the most courageous surfers, swimmers and scuba divers. It is exactly here that numerous beaches are clustered together: sand beaches next to rugged coastal cliffs or even huge blocks of volcanic rock line the coast.

Arrecife's **Playa del Reducto** is a small bay near the Gran Hotel. There, as well as at the San Gabriel Fortress are ideal places for sunbathing. The beaches are cleaned regularly. However, seaweed and other ocean rubble is often washed up on shore, which drives off some holiday visitors.

Not far from Arrecife is the settlement of **Playa Honda.** A promenade runs directly along the fine, sandy beach with a number of restaurants in which one can eat better and for less money than in most of the capital's restaurants.

A true experience is seeing the crater lake of →*El Golfo* which has an especially high salt concentration because the seawater seeps into the Lago

Verde and then evaporates – a phenomenon similar to the principle behind the salt flats of Janubio. Swimming in this lake is prohibited because this is a nature reserve area. The beach is dark in colour and protected from the wind by the crater. There is also a small beach near →*Janubio*. As is the case with all of Lanzarote's beaches, the infrastructure is not highly developed: no showers, no toilets – at most a dustbin and a number of enterprising young gentlemen who set up sunshades and beach chairs in the morning hours and then rent them out for £1.85 to £3.70 ($3.25 to $6.25).

Buses

The most important transport routes on the island are served by the "Trans-portes de Lanzarote, S.L." company. Their buses run daily on the northern, southern and central routes departing from Arrecife. The departure times listed below are subject to change. Information on schedule changes is posted in the "Transportes de Lanzarote" office in Arrecife, Calle García Escámez 71. One can also enquire by telephone, Tel: 81 15 46.

Southern Routes
Arrecife – Puerto del Carmen
Weekdays and Saturdays: 6:30, 7:30, 8:30, 9:20, 10:20 and 11:00 am; 12:20, 12:45, 1:30, 2:20, 3:30, 5:00, 6:15 and 8:15 pm.
Sundays: 6:30, 7:30, 9:20, 10:20 and 11:30 am; 1:30, 3:30, 5:00, 6:15 and 10:45 pm.
Puerto del Carmen – Arrecife
Weekdays and Saturdays: 7:30, 9:00, 9:30, 10:15, 11:15 and 11:45 am; 2:15, 4:00, 4:15, 4:30, 5:30 and 7:30 pm.
Sundays: 7:30, 9:00, 10:00 and 11:00 am; noon, 4:00, 4:15, 7:30, and 11:15 pm.
Arrecife – Playa Blanca
Weekdays and Saturdays: 6:30 am; 1:30 and 6:15 pm.
Sundays: 8:00 am; 1:30 and 10:30 pm.
Playa Blanca – Arrecife
Weekdays and Saturdays: 7:30 am; 2:45 and 7:30 pm.
Sundays: 9:30 am and 6:00 pm.

Those who seek will find: there are still a few secluded beaches to discover on Lanzarote

Northern Routes
Arrecife – Costa Teguise (Los Zocos Club Resort)
Daily: 7:15, 9:00 and 11:00 am; 2:15, 3:30, 6:00 and 8:00 pm.
Costa Teguise (Los Zocos Club Resort) – Arrecife
Daily: 8:15, 9:30 and 11:30 am; 12:30, 2:45, 4:15, 6:30 and 8:30 pm.
Arrecife – Maguez
6:30 and 11:00 am; 1:30, 6:00, 7:00, 8:00 and 8:15 pm.
The 7 pm bus does not operate on Saturdays; on Sundays or on holidays.
There is an additional bus at 7:30 pm.
Maguez – Arrecife
5:30, 7:14 and 11:45 am; 3:00 and 6:55 pm.
There are additional buses at 8:45 am and 6:45 pm on Sundays and holidays.
Arrecife – Teguise
7:00 and 1:00 am; 12:45, 1:30, 6:00, 7:00 and 8:00 pm.
The 7 pm bus does not operate on Saturdays.
Teguise – Arrecife
6:15, 8:05 and 11:20 am; 3:15, 4:15 and 6:15 pm.
The 6:15 pm bus does not operate on Saturdays.

Central Routes
Arrecife – Tinajo
6:30, 8:00 and 11:15 am; 12:30, 1:30, 6:00 and 8:00 pm.
There is an additional bus at 7 pm on Saturdays.
Tinajo – Arrecife
5:30, 8:00 and 9:00 am; noon and 3:00 pm.
There is an additional bus at 7 pm on Saturdays.
On Sundays and holidays, there are 5 additional buses at 6:30, 7:30 and 8:30
am as well as at 2:30 and 7:00 pm.
Arrecife – Soo
6:45 am; 1:30 and 7:00 pm
Soo – Arrecife
5:30 and 8:30 am and Saturdays at 3:45 pm.
Arrecife – San Bartolomé
11:30 am; 12:15 and 1:30 pm.
Additional buses on Saturday at 6:30 and 7 pm.
San Bartolomé – Arrecife
5:30, 6:15, 7:30, 8:00, 9:00 and 9:30 am; 3:15 and 7:15 pm.

Camping

On the Canary Islands, there are not many official campsites: the islands are not suited for camping. There are only three official campsites on the seven islands and these are located on Gran Canaria and Tenerife. At least one of these is equipped with showers, snack bars and electricity and is, therefore, suited to those with more discerning taste.

Those who would like to merely pitch a tent somewhere must be aware of the following: it is prohibited to pitch a tent within one kilometre (½ mile) of the coast and within 50 metres (55 yards) of the main roads. The beaches are considered everyone's; those who plan on camping out in a tent should look for a more secluded spot where he or she is not disturbed and does not disturb anyone else. If pitching a tent on a farm or private property, one must first ask permission of the owner.

Camping vehicles can be parked on public parking areas even in the larger cities without any recourse from the Policia Municipal.

One place where camping equipment should definitely be brought along when planning a longer stay is the island of →*Graciosa*. There are only a few guest houses on this island. Those who are enchanted with the solitude of Playa de las Conjas are well advised to at least bring along a sleeping bag.

Car Rental

It is definitely worthwhile to compare prices at different car rental agencies. Those offering rental cars have already adapted to this and have price lists available – sometimes under the wipers of the car itself, which one can take along on one's search. The daily rental price depends on the total length of time that the car will be rented. For example, a Seat Panda costs around £13. 30 ($25) per day if rented for three days; from four to six days, it is £12.70 ($24); and if rented for 7 or more days, the price drops to £11.70 ($22) per day. The Panda is the least expensive vehicle available to rent, but not very comfortable for tall people. A Suzuki jeep or a land rover is more comfortable to drive, but costs over twice the price of a Panda.

Upon request, personal and comprehensive insurance is available, costing around £8. 50 ($16) per day per vehicle. However, for this price, one can return to the beach quickly after a police protocol has been taken, if one should have a minor accident. This brings the price per day for a Seat Panda to around £20 to £25 ($37 to $44) per day.

One should by all means pay attention to the following:
Does the vehicle have a spare tire and tools for changing the tire? Do the turn signals, wipers, headlights and brakes function properly? Do all of the doors close securely? One must also sign a statement that the car will not be left unlocked at any time and that the vehicle was handed over in a satisfactory condition. Therefore, one should quickly check the car in the presence of the renter and make the renter aware of any deficiencies as well as any dents and scratches; this in the presence of witnesses.

Casas de Guignon → *Tinajo*
Castillo de Guanapay → *Guanapay*

Castillo de los Colorades

The Castillo de los Colorades fortress near →*Playa Blanca* consists of only ruins today. No one knows for sure anymore when exactly this fortress was built. It is located in the administrative district of Yaiza and was presumably built during the first years of the conquest, around 1402. It was here that the Spaniards coming from Fuerteventura intended to land and penetrate into the island's interior.
Since the fortress consists of only a tower today, it is also known as Torre del Aguila (Eagle's Tower). The fact that only this tower remains standing was predominantly due to African invaders who heavily damaged the fortress in 1749 during their invasions. The Torre's bell tower dates back to the 19th century.

César Manrique

The artist César Manrique suffered a shocking setback when his managers had apparently embezzled 80 million Pesetas (almost £450,000/$750,000) and the tax officials were breathing down his neck. A consultant and also a friend of his worked out a two-year plan in order to bring Manrique's business affairs in order again. Manrique said of himself that he does have money even though he didn't consider himself as being wealthy. And even he were wealthy, that wouldn't be anything bad. Manrique lives and creates for Art — and Lanzarote. Only one year after his financial misfortune he was back on top: at the end of 1987, he travelled to Japan to be celebrated as a representative of contemporary Spanish art. There, Manrique's works were compared to those of Goya and Picasso.

As reported by the island's newspaper "Lancelot", Manrique was invited to Japan by Seibu, an industrial firm with an eye for art. In an exhibition, not only were 20 works by Goya and six by Picasso from the Prado National Gallery in Madrid on display, but 40 works from different creative periods of César Manrique were shown as well. This was definitely a great honour for the artist even when he is already internationally renowned.

César Manrique feels a bond to Lanzarote as no other and seems to have a hand in just about everything on the island. Sometimes he emcees the "La Tarde" talkshow and interviews interesting personalities from the island. April 24. is his birthday which he is said to celebrate only with his closest circle of friends, which is quite extensive. At other times he can suddenly be found on Mallorca where he is being honoured for his ecological and nature preservation activities. He is co-founder of the "El Guinche" ecological organisation. During all of this, a book on the life of this artist was introduced in Heidelberg/Germany. And, when the then 22-year-old Prince Faysal of Jordan took his honeymoon trip to Lanzarote in August 1987, it was César Manrique who received the couple on the island. For César as well as for King Hussein's son, this was a memorable event.

Manrique is considered the father of this island. Even though it might sound somewhat exaggerated, the Venetian Leónardo Torriani who built the fortresses on Lanzarote and La Gomera claimed that no one had made a more significant artistic contribution to architecture than "our César", as he is called by so many.

Cheques →*Money*

Children

The most common type of holiday accommodation on the Canary Islands – bungalows and apartments – makes travelling with children much easier, although hotels welcome children as well. A local babysitter can usually be arranged through the hotel reception.

Where the beaches are not gently sloping and the water not shallow, there are usually swimming and wading pools suited to children, and sometimes even attended playgrounds. When on the beach, one should definitely be cautious of the waves when swimming with children.

Climate

The Canaries are reputed to be the "islands of eternal springtime" – at least by the tour organisations. Temperatures vary by only 7°C (13°F) from the hottest to the coldest months.

However, it does also rain, and snow can even be found in the mountains of La Palma and Tenerife. The beaches are, however, no more than a few hours away, where one can relax in the sunshine or take a stroll through the banana plantations. When travelling in summer, there is rarely a risk of bad weather. The climate is Mediterranean/subtropical. Palms, pines, sugar cane and potatoes grow only a few miles distance from each other.

On summer days, the weather can be very hot and can also be quite muggy and humid. Those travelling to the south of the island must count on a stiff breeze or even strong winds. The arid Sahara winds, the "levantes", or the haramattes blow over the islands three to four times a year, and then for up to five days. The winds transport the fine Sahara sand. It is estimated that up to 5,000 tons of sand are carried by the "levante" to Gran Canaria during the course of one year. The temperatures during this time can climb to 45°C (114°F) in the interior of the island with humidity falling under 30%.

The following are the average amounts of precipitation per year:

Island	Precipitation
Lanzarote:	135 mm
Fuerteventura:	147 mm
Gran Canaria:	325 mm
Tenerife:	420 mm
La Gomera:	410 mm
El Hierro:	426 mm
La Palma:	526 mm

In the Anaga Mountains on Tenerife and in Tamadaba on Gran Canaria, up to 1,200 millimetres of rain can fall during years with more moisture. In other years, in contrast, there is little rain at all. The pine forests in the mountainous regions extract the moisture from low-hanging clouds. In these areas, the precipitation can be up to 2,500 mm in a year.

On Tenerife, La Palma and Gran Canaria, the average temperature during the winter is 15°C (60°F); there are 6 to 10 days during a month when there is rainfall. As a result of the close proximity to the African continent and the fact that Lanzarote and Fuerteventura have no mountains, there is very little precipitation on these islands. The southern portions of the islands are drier than in the northern regions. The areas to the east of the highlands are usually cloudier. These regions are an excellent choice for a holiday during the winter or spring months; in summer, many visitors find it unbearably hot.

Climate / Lanzarote

The following table will provide an impression of the consistently mild climate of Lanzarote. The water temperature always remains between 17°C and 22°C (63°F and 72°F). At night, temperatures rarely drop below 13°C (56°F) and during the day the thermometer climbs to temperatures between 20°C and 30°C (68°F and 86°F)

Temperatures in °C (°F)	High	Low	Water
January	20 (68)	13 (55)	18 (65)
February	21 (70)	13 (55)	18 (65)
March	23 (74)	13 (55)	17 (63)
April	23 (74)	14 (57)	17 (63)
May	23 (74)	14 (57)	17 (63)
June	25 (77)	16 (61)	20 (68)
July	28 (83)	18 (65)	20 (68)
August	29 (84)	18 (65)	21 (70)
September	29 (84)	19 (66)	22 (72)
October	27 (81)	18 (65)	22 (72)
November	24 (75)	16 (61)	20 (68)
December	22 (72)	14 (57)	19 (66)

Precipitation will not prove to be a problem as long as one is on holiday and is not a local farmer. Awaiting the holiday traveller is an island characterised for the most part by perpetual sunshine. And if it does happen to rain, this is reason enough to celebrate the event with the local farmers. Rain clouds rarely hang for long above the island of Lanzarote since there are no mountains to trap them.

The only precipitation one can readily count on is the sand swept over from the Sahara by the easterly winds. This means a few days of more limited visibility but the sand settles and the island – although dusty – is back to its former sunny self.

Clothing and Equipment

On the islands of "eternal springtime", one must be prepared for any type of spring weather: during the day, it can get quite warm *(→Climate);* at night, in contrast, it can get so cool that a sweater should not be missing from anyone's luggage. Trips to the neighbouring islands of La Palma, La Gomera, El Hierro, Tenerife and Gran Canaria lead through damp and cold areas, especially when it is foggy and windy. Along the coasts and when swimming, it is appropriate to wear light tennis shoes or plastic sandals because the way to the beach is often over sharp stones or gravel.

Because the sun can be very intense, a hat and (for those with sensitive eyes) sunglasses are recommended in addition to the usual bathing equipment.

For those wishing to camp on Lanzarote: a light aluminium sleeping bag indeed takes up little space; however, it is unsuited for the relatively chilly nights on the Canary Islands. A down sleeping bag is more appropriate.

Cochenille

Some get an itchy feeling when they only hear the word "lice", others feel bad for the plants on which some species prey, still others are thankful for these small creatures because they colour the lips deep red. These are the cochineal lice.

Columbus himself is said to have been enthused with the cochineal lice which live on the broad, flat opuntia cactus. The male of this species can fly and grows from 1.6 to 2 mm. The male's fate is sealed after he pairs with a female – he dies. Fourteen days later, the female lays eggs and covers these with a fine web. The larvae develop within this web which are the actual suppliers of the carmesine pigment.

The harvest of the lice is becoming increasingly rationalised. Today, fertilised females are collected in a sack. This is then hung on a cactus plant and the females lay their eggs on the cactus through the sack cloth. The larvae are then killed in hot water, dried and roasted. The pigments are activated through a chemical process and then used in the production of lipstick and cosmetics. Centres for cochineal breeding are Mala and Guatiza *(→Vegetation).*

During the 19th century, the opuntia cactus was broght to the islands and with this, the cochineal lice

Conduct

The golden rule is always applicable: do unto others as you would have them do unto you. The guest, even when paying for the time spent on Tenerife, should respect his or her host. Although this should go without saying, there are always discouraging scenes, especially at the bus stops. Visitors push and shove.

In some of the more expensive hotels, it is common practice to wear a tie. Those who do as the Romans when in Rome will also wear a tie during the evening meal. When visiting a church, a tie cannot hurt either. It would be completely out of context to visit the old, beautiful churches in shorts or – God forbid – in a bikini. A bikini is appropriate for the beach or the swimming pool. Otherwise it should be left in the closet – and it certainly should not be worn in museums or stores.

Topless swimming and sunbathing is tolerated on most of the beaches. Swimming completely nude is possible, but only on those beaches specifically set apart for this. Those who find themselves among Canarians, whose wives and daughters are wearing a bathing suit or bikini should react appropriately and forgo taking everything off.

Alcohol is considered a "demon" that should be kept under control, even when it is so inexpensive in this duty-free zone. Unfortunately, some visitors take advantage of the prices; barroom brawls and street fights are the results – a loss of control that could have easily been avoided.

The Spanish police should never become the brunt of jokes, ridicule or harassment. Their patent leather hat is merely a part of the uniform. Remaining objective and factual when confronted by an official is appropriate, and one should follow their instructions. This can solve the avoidable problem of having one's holiday "officially" shortened.

→ _Tipping, Nudity_

Costa Teguise

Around 6 kilometres (4½ miles) from the centre of Arrecife is the Costa Teguise complex. It was named after the former capital of Lanzarote which is located north of Arrecife.

The architect and nature conservationalist César Manrique was decisive in the development of this town. He and another architect, a friend of his, actually designed this settlement and built the luxury hotel at the centre with numerous plants both inside and surrounding the hotel. This encouraged other companies to also move to this area. In only a short time, one of the largest holiday complexes on Lanzarote came into being here. César Manrique's hotel is a work of art in which one can live (→*Accommodation);* without this hotel, Costa Teguise would not even exist. This trademark of the island attracts many thousands of holiday travellers to this region of the island every year. Manrique has now turned to new projects and left Costa Teguise to his successors. This area has long, lightly coloured sand beaches, provides the opportunity to surf and also offers good shopping in the numerous shops within this holiday resort. Evening entertainment and dancing predominantly takes place in the hotel. The golf course shortly beyond the entrance to Costa Teguise on the left-hand side has 18 holes and is popular with both experienced golfers and novices around the world.

This golf course is open to the public from 9 am to 6 pm and between 9 am and 5 pm one can polish up one's swing and stance on the practice course with golf trainers. Guests who are not staying in the resort complex pay around £14 ($24), those staying in the complex pay around £11 ($19); £4. 50 ($7. 50) is charged for children under 14. The prices become more reasonable when booking for seven days, then the greens fees cost around £77 ($132); for club members, £60 ($104), Club rules prohibit golfing without a shirt or in swimwear.

Costa Teguise / **Practical Information**

Accommodation

The pearl among the hotels on Costa Teguise is the "Las Salinas Sol" Hotel (*****), Costa Teguise, Tel: 81 30 40. A true experience when staying here and guests might just not ever want to leave, given the appropriate travel budget. The hotel has a heated pool, fitness rooms, bars, the "El Majo" discotheque, shops, tennis and volleyball courts to name only a few of the facilities this hotel has to offer. The reception hall is overwhelming: green everywhere with the rush of artificial waterfalls. Parents can leave their children to play in the play corner where they are attended to.

The "Las Salinas Sol" has 591 fully air conditioned rooms with marble baths. A single room is priced at £91 ($157) without breakfast; a double room, from £113 ($194). A rollaway bed for children from two to twelve years of age is available for £37 ($63). One consolation for those who can't afford any of this: there is no charge for extra cushions.

The "Teguise Playa" Hotel (****), Urbanización Costa Teguise, Tel: 81 11 30, is the attempt to copy the concept behind "Las Salinas Sol". It has 325 rooms with a view of the sea; tennis and squash courts, a sauna, a fitness studio, shops and is only 3 kilometres (2 miles) from the golf course. Double rooms start at £55 ($94) without breakfast.

Aparthotel "Los Zocos"; a generously laid out complex with tennis courts and swimming pools. 244 apartments.

Apartment House "Las Cucharas" (three keys), Costa Teguise. 69 apartments priced from £18 ($32).

Apartment House "Los Molinos" (three keys), Costa Teguise, Tel: 81 20 12. 126 Apartments priced from £33 ($57).

Car Rental

Autos Cabrera Medina, Apartamentos Las Cucharas, Tel: 81 35 73.

Cueva de los Verdes

Cueva de los Verdes, the underground cavern in the lava fields of Malpaises de Corona north of Arrieta once served as a hideout for the natives of Lanzarote, first from the Spaniards and then from the pirates who came from Europe or Africa to attack the island.

The Cueva de los Verdes is accessible by driving from Arrieta in the northern regions of Lanzarote keeping right and following the signs along the coastal road. From Mirador del Rio in the northern portions of Lanzarote, one must drive southeast via Ye to Llanos and then turn left at the sign after around 6 kilometres (4 miles). The one-lane road with widenings to accommodate the oncoming traffic leads directly through the wastelands of Malpaises. Malpais means as much as "badlands" and these cooled lava fields can hardly even support plant life.

After around 2 kilometres (1¼ miles) on the narrow roadway one hardly expects anything – then suddenly one finds oneself on a parking area. Unnoticable from this vantage point, the masses of lava have formed a network of caves underground which consists of 7 kilometres (4½ miles) of passageways leading to the exit at Jameos del Agua.

The Cueva de los Verdes can be toured daily from 11 am to 6 pm. For around £4 ($3) the multi-lingual guides lead visitors through this fascinating underground world. Since the number of visitors can number more than 50, one must be sure to keep close to the guide to understand his explanations.

The route covered in around 45 minutes is around 2 kilometres (1¼ miles) long. The ceiling of the highest hall called the "cathedral" reaches a height of 50 metres (164 feet) and consists of several hollow layers of lava. These passageways are called "galerías" interesting formations developed as the lava flow cooled: a "piano" can be seen as well as a tree stump, Queen Victoria and the Iranian leader Ayatollah Khomeini.

Then the corridor suddenly opens to a spacious room which serves as a concert hall which is completely isolated from outside noise. The television stations were often here to broadcast performances by singers and musicians. Just as fascinating as surprising is the "lake" in one of the halls. Since no sunlight can penetrate from outside, the ceiling of this hall is reflected on the waters surface. Even if one is aware of this, one will still approach the water cautiously since it seems as if one is standing before an abyss around 30 metres (98 feet) deep. The illusion is quickly broken by tossing a stone into the "abyss". The water is only a few inches deep.

Cuisine

Some view it as a custom, others consider it unhealthy nutrition: on the "islands of happiness" dinner is eaten quite late in the day. The Canarians rarely eat their noonday meal before 2 pm. Dinner (the evening meal) is usually not served before 8 pm. Tourism has confused these traditions somewhat, and in the larger resort cities, visitors can eat at those times to which they are accustomed (→ *Time of Day*).

A Canarian breakfast consists of a type of deep-fried dough which is dipped into coffee or tea. In the hotels, however, continental breakfast (with bread rolls, ham and cheese) as well as English breakfast (with bacon and eggs and breakfast cereals) is served.

In the restaurants, European cuisine is also served. More typically Canarian cuisine can usually be found in the more remote village pubs, called "Fondas", "Tascas" or simply bars. The following are examples of what one can order:

tapas: snacks like slices of salami or cheese
paella: sometimes quite spicy, this is steamed rice in vegetable oil with prawns, mussels, different types of fish, shrimps and chicken
potaje de veduras: thick vegetable soup
escaldon: a thick, pulpy soup with gofio
gofio: a bread-like, deep-fried pastry, most tasty when served fresh or toasted.
caldo: beef bouillon
sopa: soup with meat or sausage
gazpacho: cold vegetable soup
sopa de mariscos: mussel soup

patates: sweet potatoes
papas arrugadas: shrunken pickled potatoes
queso blanco: goat's cheese
vino tinto: red wine
cuba libre: cola with locally produced rum
sangria: wine with fruit, also called "the liquid hangover"
cafe solo: dark roasted coffee
cafe con leche: coffee with milk

For Recipes → *Appendix*

Culture

Those who are not particularly interested in Stone Age relics will be disappointed in what remains of the original culture of the Canary Islands: the Guanches left only mummies, skulls and pieces of pottery behind for the museums.

What is noticeably better represented are remnants of the Canarian culture, documenting the development after the conquest of the islands:

The historical buildings on the Canary Islands contain gothic, renaissance and baroque elements. Statues of the Virgen Mary like La Virgen de Teror en Gran Canaria, the Nuestra Señora de las Nieves on La Palma and the Virgen de Candelaria are among the most important depictions of the mother of God. Visitors will note the similarity between the El Salvador Church in Santa Cruz de La Palma and other European cathedrals like the cathedral in Cologne or between the Virgen de Candelaria and the cherubs in Paris' Louvre. The richly embellished balconies and ceilings built from Canarian pine are reminiscent of southern Spain.

The combination of Gothic and intricate Moorish elements in the "Mudejar" style was foremost practised by artisans and craftsmen with Arabian heritage, who were converted to the Christian faith between the 13th and 15th centuries. Their horseshoe arches, ceiling and majolica ornamentation and a wealth of geometrical designs in these forms can also be found on the Canary Islands. The plateresque style is termed as the "goldsmith" style (Spanish: "plateresco") even though the works of art are not made of metal but are carved from wood.

Those who tactfully wander into the inner courtyards of the residential houses will be pleasantly surprised: the patios are lovingly decorated with plants and the stairways are especially pretty.

Currency →*Money*

Customs Regulations

Upon entry, there are no customs limitations in the duty-free zone of the Canary Islands. One must, however, pay attention to the Spanish customs regulations when travelling from the Canaries to the Spanish mainland.
When returning to the United Kingdom, one may bring along 200 cigarettes or 50 cigars or 250 grams of tobacco as well as 1 litre of spirits and 2 litres of wine.
When returning to the United States, one may bring along 200 cigarettes and 100 cigars and a reasonable amount of tobacco as well as 1 litre of spirits or 1 litre of wine.

Customs and Traditions   →*Conduct, Folklore, Culture, Holidays and Celebrations*

Discounts

Children under 14 pay half the adult fare when using public transportation (buses and boats); children under 4 ride free. As a rule, the same is true for admission to amusement parks. If uncertain, one should definitely ask.
International car rental agencies such as Europcar, Avis and Hertz grant members of their clubs discounts of up to 25% off the normal rental price. It is, however, still worth comparing prices: an Opel Corsa or Ascona is, as a general rule, always more expensive than a Seat Panda, which are frequently offered by local rental agencies at low prices (→*Car Rental*).

Distances

When planning day trips, one can easily underestimate the distances on Lanzarote: the maps (→*Maps)* usually include no distances, or those included are inexact. The longest distances on this island can be covered in a matter of a few hours on good roads; exact distances will, however, prove helpful. A visit to the capital should definitely be included in one's holiday plans on

Lanzarote. Therefore, the distances between Arrecife and the most important places are listed here:

Airport—7 km (4½ miles)	Montañas
Arrieta—24 km (15 miles)	del Fuego—34 km (21 miles)
Cueva de los Verdes—30 km	Mozaga—11 km (7 miles)
(19 miles)	Nazaret—9 km (6 miles)
El Golfo—32 km (20 miles)	Orzola—37 km (23 miles)
Famara—5 km	Papagayo Beaches—50 km
(15½ miles)	(31 miles)
Guatiza—16 km (10 miles)	Playa Blanca—40 km (25 miles)
Güime—16 km (10 miles)	Playa Honda—5 km (3 miles)
Haría—30 km (19 miles)	Puerto del Carmen—15 km
Jameos del Agua—30 km	(9½ miles)
(19 miles)	San Bartolomé—9 km (6 miles)
Janubio—30 km (19 miles)	Soo 21 km—(13 miles)
La Caleta—25 km	Tahiche 7 km—(4½ miles)
(15½ miles)	Tao 14 km—(9 miles)
La Vagueta—18 km	Teguise 12 km—(7½ miles)
(11¼ miles)	Tiagua—16 km (10 miles)
Las Breñas—32 km (20 miles)	Tias—12 km (7½ miles)
Las Caletas—9 km (6 miles)	Tinajo—20 km (12½ miles)
Macher—15 km (9 miles)	Uga 20 km (13 miles)
Mirador del Rio—37 km	Yaiza 23 km (14 miles)
(23 miles)	Ye 35 km (22 miles).

Economy

The most important branches of the economy are (in addition to tourism) agriculture and the fishing industry, as has been the case for centuries. In historical times, the pigments of orchilla and orseille (Rocella tinctoria) used in the production of purple dyes played a significant economic role on the eastern Canary Islands (→*History*).

In the 19th century, the opuntias were introduced, and with them, the cochineal, a louse, whose purple pigment "Carmine" is still used in the production of lipstick which later colours the lips red (→*Vegetation*).

Fishing (especially anchovies and tuna) is concentrated between Fuerteventura, Lanzarote and the African continent. These waters are also fished by a large proportion of foreign fishing fleets. The Canarians fish mainly to cover domestic demand.

The harbours of Las Palmas and Tenerife continue to gain importance. In Santa Cruz de Tenerife, there is even an oil refinery.

Canarian cigars are produced in small tobacco factories in Las Palmas de Gran Canaria, Santa Cruz de Tenerife and Santa Cruz de La Palma, which can compete with their counterparts from Havana.

In 1974, 400,000 metric tons of bananas were produced on 12,000 hectares of cultivated land, 90% of which were exported to the Spanish mainland. The Canaries have the advantage that the distance to the shipping harbours is always short. This makes it possible for even sensitive fruits like the Indonesian or Cavendish banana to reach the consumer quickly. The Canary Islands also produced 135,000 metric tons of tomatoes on an area of 7,000 hectares (17,500 acres) in 1974. These were mainly exported countries other than Spain in Western Europe. In the moist, cloudy regions in the north and central regions of Gran Canaria, potatoes are the main crop. The potato crops on the Canary Islands can be harvested twice a year.

Tobacco, onions and sweet potatoes are harvested on La Palma and Lanzarote as well. Green peppers and cucumbers thrive in the green-houses; egg-plants in the irrigated fields. Also growing in the greenhouses of the Canaries are roses, chrysanthemums and carnations for the export market. An area of 425 hectares (1,063 acres) of the islands is used in gardening.

Sugar cane, which played an important role in the 18th century, has become an insignificant economical factor today. Only in the northern regions of Gran Canaria is rum produced from the sugar cane grown on this island.

Grapes for the production of the excellent Canarian red and light muscatel wines are grown on Lanzarote and Gran Canaria (El Monte, in the Tafira region). Another well known wine is the malvasia, produced on Lanzarote, El Hierro and La Palma. The production of wines has, however, decreased dramatically since the 19th century when mildew destroyed a large proportion of the grapevines.

The Canary Islands are geographically fascinating. However, visitors must often hike for hours to see the points of geographical interest. Inevitably, they will also come upon the evidence of unfamiliar agricultural methods:

"secano" is the Canarian term for the farming of an irrigated field. A special type of agricultural technique is called "enarenando," the non-irrigated method, where plants are placed in 200 to 800 shallow funnels per hectare, for example on Tenerife and especially often on Lanzarote. Then is also the method of covering the ground with grey pumice called "jable" in the sand dunes of

Lanzarote. Mixing the soil with yellow pumice is termed "sahorra." The reason for this is to absorb warmth during the day, whereby the soil then quickly cools in the evening, collecting the condensation. The plants thrive as if in a greenhouse, the humus protected from the wind by pumice and earthen retaining walls.

Crops cultivated using the "enarenando" method are corn, potatoes, yams, tomatoes, tobacco, grapes, barley, oats, alfalfa, most of the fruit trees and opuntias. The "jable" method, used in the southern regions of Tenerife between Granadilla, Vilaflor and San Miguel – or on extensive tracts of land on Lanzarote – is employed in cultivating wheat, barley, tomatoes, water-melons and cucumbers.

The "sahorra" method allows for up to four harvests on the same fields per year on El Hierro: tomatoes between August and December; potatoes between December and March and again around May; corn up until August.

El Golfo

If continuing farther on the main road through Yaiza, one will reach an intersection after around 2 kilometres (1¼ miles). To the left, the main road continues towards Janubio and Playa Blanca; to the left a gravel road leads past the lava and gravel fields to El Golfo. This unpaved roadway is bumpy and reminiscent of a washboard in places. It is a very adventuresome drive. Growing on the gravel fields to both sides of the roadway are lichens and mosses; scattered among these are also a few cactus fields. After travelling 4 kilometres (2 miles), one will reach El Golfo. A second route leads along the coast through Janubio passing by Montaña Bermeja. The coastal road to El Golfo is paved. There are parking areas at the widenings in the road with eroded volcanic rock formations.

El Golfo is famous for its huge half-crater filled with water with a high concentration of salt. A sand barrier protects the natural swimming pool from drying up. Sea water continually seeps into the basin, but the impression of a "dead sea" remains. The lake is named Lago Verde because it shimmers in shades of green. It is still possible to take a stroll along the long black beaches; however, swimming in the lake is not. The lake has declared a nature reserve. With the exception of directly along the crater, the coast of El Golfo is rugged and windy.

This quaint village served as the backdrop for the Italian-American film "La Iguana" based on the work by the Spanish author Alberto Vasquez Figuera.

Restaurants: There are various bars and restaurants directly along the coast which open late in the afternoon. These include "Siroco", "La Choza", "Casa Victorio" and "Mar Azul". The dining room in "Mar Azul" offers a magnificent view of this town's gulf and coastline. All of the restaurants can be especially recommended for their fish dishes.

El Rubicon

El Rubicon is the plain west of Playa Blanca and south of the Salinas of Janubio. It was from here that the Norman Jean de Bethancourt attempted to conquer Fuerteventura during the 15th century *(→History)*.

Electricity

The voltage on the Canary Islands varies: sometimes it is 110 to 125 volts alternating current, in the tourist centres, 220 volts. Those who do not want to forgo bringing their electric shaver or blow dryer, should take this into consideration. The appropriate sockets are also not always available. An adapter should, therefore, be brought along.

Embassies and Consulates

British Embassy
Calle Fernando el Santo 16
Madrid, Spain
Tel: 4 19 15 28
Santa Cruz de Tenerife
British Consulate
Calle de Suárez Guerra 40
Santa Cruz de Tenerife
Tel: 24 20 00

Canadian Embassy
Calle Nuñez de Balboa 35
Madrid, Spain
Tel: 4 31 43 00
United States Embassy
Calle Serrano 75
Madrid, Spain
Tel: 2 76 36 00,
emergenciy Tel: 2 76 32 29

Entertainment

The Canary Islands have everything from discotheques to night clubs and even sports facilities and excursions – everything that will augment an enjoyable holiday. To avoid misunderstandings, here are a few general remarks:

A "restaurante" is a restaurant. A "bar" is not necessarily a night club but a café, a snack bar, or a wine bar serving wine directly from the barrel.

The atmosphere in night clubs and discotheques first picks up around midnight. Folklore and singing groups usually do not begin their performances until 11 pm – but then they last until around 3 am. The Canarian music has Andalusian and South American elements. The "islas" are ironic; the "folias", emotional; the "arroros", sentimental; and the "canarios" are lively, vibrant songs. The latter are so popular that even Louis XIV had them performed in his court.

Both the provincial capitals of Las Palmas de Gran Canaria and Santa Cruz de Tenerife have theatres. The Teatro de Guimera in Santa Cruz de Tenerife (Calle Imeldo Seris), as well as the Teatro Perez Galdos (Calle Triana) in Las Palmas de Gran Canaria, are the most widely known, in which predominantly operas are performed.

Ermita de las Nieves

The GC 730 road leads from Teguise past Castillo Guanapay in the northern regions of Lanzarote. 10 kilometres (6¼ miles) from Teguise, a track leads off into the Vista de las Nieves massif. At the summit is the chapel of Ermita de las Nieves massif. The Ermita de las Nieves Chapel is perched atop the summit.

From this highland plateau one can see all the way from El Jable to Playa de Famara near La Caleta. One can even recognise the La Isleta peninsula and Teguise during clear weather. The highland plateau near the chapel offers the best panorama on the entire island.

Famara-Guatifay →*La Caleta*
Faro Pechiguera →*Punta Pechiguera*

Femés

Femés lies at the base of the Atalaya de Femés massif reaching an elevation of 608 metres (1,988 feet).

It is situated halfway between Janubio and Uga in the southwestern portion of Lanzarote and is accessible via an auxiliary road passing by La Breñas.

The town is laid out on an elevation. Next to the San Pedro Church is a bar. In some other sources, the church is also referred to as "San Marcial de Rubicon" or "Emerita del San Marcial".

The church was so named in commemoration of a cardinal who is said to have brought Jean de Bethancourt to Lanzarote during the 15th century.

There are also public telephones available in this town. Behind the "Femés" bar, a handicrafts shop called "Artesanía Canaria" sells pottery and baskets. There is a postbox next to the small shop on the main street.

Femés is an old city which evolved over centuries on Lanzarote with around 30 buildings. The residents make their living from orange plantations and grow maize (corn) and grain which is protected from the arid climate with dark pumice.

Ferries → *Travelling on Lanzarote, Travel to Lanzarote*

A habitat for the cochineal lice: opuntia fields as far as the eye can see

Folklore

The painter Nestor de la Torre (in whose honour the Museo Nestor in Las Palmas de Gran Canaria was built) designed colourful costumes according to old, almost forgotten patterns at the beginning of the 20th century. These costumes are still worn on all of the Canary Islands as folklore costumes during "Canarian Evenings" and festivals.

These evenings are organised by almost every tour organisation or one can inquire at the travel agencies in the tourist centres or in larger hotels.

The songs play the most prominent role in these performances. Love is the most popular theme which is presented sometimes ironically, sometimes romantically. The lyrics are accompanied by the small "timple" similar to a guitar and typical for Canarian music.

According to the legends handed down on the Canary Islands, the Guanches and Spaniards made less of a historical and literary mark than did the Greeks. The Greek sagas claim that the Canary Islands are the remains of the sunken city of Atlantis. According to another story, the gardens of Hesperides were found on these islands – gardens where the apples of eternal youth could be found. When considering that apples do not grow here and that the Canary Islands have a number of beautiful cemeteries, this legend must remain a legend.

Although people still do find their final resting place on these islands, they make the most of life up until this time. This is reflected by the saying "Salud, amor y dinero – y el tiempo para gozarlo", meaning "health, love and money – and time enough to enjoy it all." And part of enjoying life is eating well. A staple is "Gofio" *(→Cuisine),* of which the men claim: gofio gives us the energy that women take.

Geography

Many islands, many worlds – highly appropriate to the Canary Islands. Tenerife was once called the "flower island", although this was linguistic plagiarism: "Flores" is the name of an island in the Azores with a large amount of precipitation, dense vegetation and the profuse flowers which give the island its name. However, neither Tenerife nor Gran Canaria pale in comparison. Due to their climatic zones and geography, Domingo Cardenes even called the latter "continente en miniatura" – a continent in miniature.

The Canary Islands are located between 27°37° (Punta Restinga on El Hierro) and 29°23° (Alegranza Island) northern latitude and 13°20° (Roque del Este) and 18°16° (Punta Orchilla on El Hierro) western longitude in the region of northwestern Africa.

Owing to this location in the Atlantic, the wind is never perfectly calm: either the haramatte winds blow over from the African continent in the east or the trade-winds from over the Atlantic in the west.

This archipelago lies at the same latitude as the sunny paradise of Florida or Egypt. It can also get quite dry here: the irrigated arable land on the Canary Islands is estimated at about 3 to 6% of the total surface, 18% for non-irrigated farming. 44% is pastureland or forests; the rest of the area is unproductive.

The Canary Islands extend over 500 kilometres (315 miles) from east to west. The shortest distance to the African continent – a little over 100 kilometres (63 miles) – is measured from Cape Juby on Fuerteventura. The islands are 1,100 kilometres (692 miles) from Gibraltar and about 4,000 kilometres (2,516 miles) from Central Europe.

Reports differ as to the exact size of the Canary Islands, varying up to 700 square kilometres (270 square miles). The Consejo Economico Social Sindical de Canarias (CESSCAN) calculated the area of all islands from Lanzarote (Alegranza) at the northeastern tip to El Hierro, the southwestern most extreme at 7,466 square kilometres (2,883 square miles) in 1973.

With only 80 kilometres (50 miles) of ocean separating them, Tenerife and Gran Canaria make up the centre of the archipelagos. La Gomera, El Hierro and La Palma surround these two main islands. La Gomera is only 23 kilometres (15 miles) from Tenerife, 60 to 65 kilometres (38 to 42 miles) separate the three western islands.

The flat eastern islands of Lanzarote and Fuerteventura make a geographical unit. They are 85 kilometres (54 miles) from Gran Canaria and run almost parallel to the African Coast. Their direct neighbours are the Isletas: located between Fuerteventura and Lanzarote is Lobos; north of Lanzarote are Graciosa, Alegranza, Montaña Clara, Roque del Este and Roque del Oeste. These islands are not all inhabited, but some do in part serve as pastureland. Lanzarote and Fuerteventura are also called the "purple islands" because a fungus used in the production of purple dyes was found here. The islands to the west are distinguished from the others by the term "Fortunatas" from the Latin "insulae fortunatae" meaning "islands of good fortune". The vegetation is described as macronesic, which comes from the Greek meaning no more than "the flora of the islands of good fortune".

The eastern islands are on Africa's continental shelf, the others were formed by volcanic activity without being on the continental shelf. With this, the hypothesis that the Canary Islands were the remnants of the legendary sunken city of Atlantis was disproved. The western islands have nothing in common, geographically speaking.

All of the islands do have three factors in common: the eroding action of flowing water, the abrasive activity of the ocean's surf and, above all, volcanism. This is how the slopes consisting of blankets of lava in varying thickness were formed. These are composed of volcanic rock, black basalt, acidic lava like andesite and trachyte, light pumice and old, charred soil – the bright red "almagre". Sometimes, one can find caves in the canyon walls or walls of basalt and phonolyte on the islands, the most significant characteristic of which is the columnar structure.

The world of volcanic formations is characterised mainly by two shapes. The linear volcano, formed by a chain of volcanic activity and the conic or cauldron volcano. The former is a type of volcano which built up along a crevice – a chain of smaller volcanoes. This type of volcano makes clear that the Canary Islands, like the Azores, belong to a fault system cutting through the middle Atlantic ridge from east-southeast to west-northwest. The most common volcanic formation on the Canary Islands is without question the "caldera" volcano, a type of cauldron crater that presumably originates from the explosion or collapse of the original volcanic cone. A lake is commonly found in the basin of this type of crater.

The Canary Islands are presumed to have been formed around 20 million years ago, whereby the eastern islands of Fuerteventura and Lanzarote are possibly even older. Found here were the fossilised eggs of prehistoric land bird also capable of flight and similar to an ostrich. The Canary Islands are at least closely related to the African continent and the theory that they were connected to the continent by a land bridge cannot be disproven. Fossilised bones of a giant lizard were also found on Tenerife. Fossilised impressions of plant life like pines and laurel stems on Gran Canaria and Tenerife are dated at 600,000 years.

Lanzarote, Tenerife and La Palma were still sights of volcanic activity in recorded history. On Gran Canaria, Fuerteventura and possibly on El Hierro eruptions could have occurred in the late prehistoric era. On La Gomera, eruptions occurred up to the start of the Quarternary Period.

See the table on the following page for a list of documented eruptions on the Canaries.

Lanzarote Geography

Lanzarote remains an island worth discovering geographically speaking. This island offers wide beaches with volcanic sand and are considered as having

Recorded Eruptions	1909 Chinyero Volcano
	La Palma:
Tenerife	1585 Volcano ce los Llanos
1393 and 1399	1677 Tigalate Volcano
1430 and 1484	1677 Fuencaliente Volcano
1492 (reported in Christopher Columbus' logbook	1705 or 1725 Charco Volcano
	1949 Volcano de las Manchas
1604 Siete Fuentes Volcano	1971 Tenegui Volcano
1606 Fasnia Volcano	
1704 Güimar Volcano	**Lanzarote:**
1705 Güimar Volcano	1824 eruptions reported at the Volcanos of Tao, Nueva del Fuego and Tinguation
1706 Garachico Volcano	
1798 Cahorra Volcano	

a "sunshine guarantee" (→*Climate*). The wind conditions attract wind surfers the world over. The craters on the island paint Lanzarote's profile as dark and untamed. The desert-like portions surrounding the villages leave a barren impression; and still: farmers coax grain, fruit and even grapes for wine out of this seemingly unfertile soil. The splotches of green in the landscape when the seeds germinate are beautiful against the backdrop of the whitewashed houses.

Expansive lava fields and almost 300 volcanic caves characterise the profile of this island with an area of 795 square kilometres (310 square miles), home to around 50,000 residents and its capital city, Arrecife. Off the northern coast of Lanzarote are the Isletas, the small islands of La Graciosa, Montaña Clara, Roque del Oeste (or Roque del Infierno), Alegranza and Roque del Este. These are in part uninhabited.

The volcanic cones rise 400 to 600 metres (1,310 to 1960 feet) which verge on the Famara-Guatifay mountains near *La Caleta* to the north and the Los Ayaches mountains to the south. The highest elevation is the eroded peak of the Peñas de Chache in the Famara chain. The northern mountain range falls off steeply to the western El Rio strait. The southern slopes are bordered by the →*El Rubicon* coastal plains. Larger valleys can only be found to the east toward the sea.

The volcanic Montaña del Fuego de Timanfaya chain came into being during eruptions which took place from 1730 to 1736. In 1824, the Tinguanton volcano then also erupted. Powerful detonations and saltwater fountains from three craters shook the island. Obviously, there was a geologic connection between the centre of the volcano and the ocean.

In 1840, forty volcanoes erupted simultaneously. The temperature under the surface of some portions of the island *(→Montañas del Fuego, Islote de Hilario)* still climbs to 400 or even 425°C (750 to 800°F) today, making it possible to fry an egg in the sand or – a popular game with tourists – to light a scrap of paper on fire. In the centre portion of the island is a 3 to 5 kilometre (2 to 3 mile) long band of sand which was formerly a region of wandering sand dunes most of which have now been anchored.

Extensive regions of the northernmost of the Canary Islands has been transformed into a type of lunar landscape since the volcanic eruptions of the 18th century. The petrified lava flows to the north are similar to red mountains of fire. One wouldn't expect anything to grow at all in these regions. Still, there are vineyards and tomato fields.

The rugged beauty of Lanzarote is especially popular for holidays on the beach. It is foremost the flat southern coast which attracts thousands of visitors. On the whole Lanzarote makes a rather surreal and untamed impression with black lava fields and dark brown sand. The name of Lanzarote's capital city of Arrecife can be traced back to the reefs off the coast. These protect the harbour and simultaneously make it easier for fishermen to build bays used to bring their catch on shore.

Golfo *→El Golfo*

Graciosa

Graciosa – also called La Graciosa – is an island off the northern coast of Lanzarote which is separated from the main island by a narrow strait called El Rio. The main town on this island is called Caleta de Sebo and readily compares to a north African desert town being surrounded by sand and playing host to only a handful of visitors.

There is no organised tourism to Graciosa; at most a few determined visitors arrive to spend a night or have a meal. At most, they spend one or two nights at one of the few guest houses. To ensure that the island never becomes overrun or outright destroyed by an influx of tourists *→César Manrique* played a key role in having this island declared a nature reserve.

There is one telephone which is property of the island; its number, 84 00 93 and no private calls are permitted. The corridor in which it is located is constantly filled with those sharing in the joys and pains of that person lucky enough to get a connection.

Graciosa is considered an island for gourmets even though there are only four bar-restaurantes which cannot be overlooked in the centre of Caleta de Sebas *(see below)*. The island is accessible by taking the "Maria del Pino" ferry from the Orzola harbour. The fare is 1,200 pesetas. Departure times: Graciosa – Orzola 10:30 am, 4 and 5:30 pm; Orzola – Graciosa 10 am, 3:30 and 5 pm. Ferries do not operate during bad weather. One can find out whether or not the weather is too bad for the crossing by calling the above mentioned island telephone.

The most common means of transportation on Graciosa is the dromedary. It is also worthwhile to get around "per pedes" in the northern portions of the island. Optically speaking, the Playa de las Conchas beach has a Caribbean flair. One must be cautious, however, when swimming here due to the dangerous currents; the undertow in some places can easily sweep swimmers out to sea. For this reason, it is better to only wade out in the water and enjoy the solitude on this beach with its fine, light sand. It is especially peaceful here in August when only a few tourists are underway.

Graciosa / **Practical Information**

Accommodation

It is best to bring along camping equipment to the island of Graciosa. A sleeping bag alone will prove sufficient because it rains only seldom here. There are three guest houses on the island, charging around £9 ($15.50) for two persons per night:

"Girasol Playa" Guest House, Calle García Escámez 1.

"Enriqueta" Guest House, near "Girasol Playa".

"Juan Romero Morales" Guest House, somewhat further into town.

The captain of the "Maria del Pino" ferry will be able to provide more information. One can also ask in the "El Marinero" bar.

Currency Exchange: Caja Insular de Ahorros en la Isla de La Graciosa, Tel: 84 00 93.

Restaurants: There are four restaurants on Graciosa which proves sufficient for the number of visitors to the island. One favourite is the "Enriqueta" bar and guest house, Tel: 84 00 93.

Shopping: Graciosa has one supermarket. The prices are somewhat higher than on the main island of Lanzarote; however, transport costs are also higher, making this understandable. Fresh bread can be found at the island's bakery.

Guanapay

Guanapay is a mountain west of the old city of Teguise. The architect Leónardo Torriani, the "Manrique of the 16th century", completed work on a fortress atop this mountain in 1596.

Originally, it was called "Castillo de Santa Barbara"; today, it is better known as "Castillo de Guanapay".

The fortress is accessible via a narrow roadway given that it is not blocked off due to maintenance work. The roadway to the fortress from Teguise is excellent.

The history of the fortress goes back to the Genovan adventurer Lanceloto Malocello, after whom the island of Lanzarote was named. Lanceloto had the fortress built in the middle of the 14th century. It was then heavily damaged by invaders but was then repaired and expanded by Captain Argote de Molina.

The bizarre lava landscapes on Lanzarote are evidence of the forces released by a volcanic eruption

Guanches

It is almost impossible to avoid contact with the Guanche culture in some way or other on the Canary Islands, nor would one want to avoid this. This group of people have not only left behind relics like mummified corpses, caves and pieces of pottery but also a marked influence on the language.

Those Canarians who are tall with light coloured hair and blue eyes might likely be able to trace their ancestry back to the original inhabitants of the Canary Islands.

The fortunate islands, "insulae fortunatae" were such a paradise that they were not only of interest to the Romans or Greeks. In 1400 BC, it is said that the Egyptian king Sesostris visited the Guanches on this group of islands. The fact that there were actually islands in the Atlantic was something that the world would once more forget – this, with the exception of the Guanches. And they, on the other hand, were not aware the world beyond the limits of their islands. They had no boats. It was only in the 15th century that this limited

An almost untouched landscape can be found on the island of Graciosa, best explored by hiking

perception of the world was questioned. The French arrived at this time to be followed somewhat later by the Spaniards. Their visit was a loud, clear and deadly signal: they arrived heavily armed. These were after all the conquerors (→*History*).

What the conquerors were to find on the island was a Stone Age culture in which pottery techniques were quite advanced although basic, and the weapons simple. With the arrival of the Spaniards on the Canary Islands, the original inhabitants would soon become known as the Guanches. This term is only really applicable to the people of Tenerife, the island which was originally called "Guancherfe". "Quan" was Guanche for "a son " and this, not any son but a son of this island. The Spaniards killed many Guanches; others, they married. The dragon which was presumed to guard the islands of bliss, the islands of Hesperides, is long since forgotten – unless it is sleeping somewhere under the surface of this volcanic island. Only a few words and phrases remain of the Guanche language.

The king had the say on the islands. If a conflict were to develop, then it would probably have to do with the rights to the land which were allocated to the farmers and shepherds. The aristocracy owned sheep, goats, pigs and rabbits. Farmers' wives worked the fields with tools made of obsidian, a volcanic, glass-like mineral.

If the fields were overcultivated, this did not concern the farmers – they did not even irrigate them. It was far simpler to move on and find a new, fertile tract of land. Those who did not want to farm or tend livestock, could earn their livelihood through fishing. The fish were driven into the bays and then bludgeoned with sticks. The Guanches were predominantly vegetarians, eating for the most part vegetables and Gofio.

The grain for Gofio was roasted, ground and then extended with water, goat's milk or lard and then spun in a goat leather bag until the proper doughy consistency was achieved. This could be eaten raw or dissolved in warm water. Today, Gofio is still a nutritious staple in the Canarian diet, made from freshly roasted grain.

Guatiza

The village of Guatiza lies 2 kilometres (1¼ miles) south of Mala in Lanzarote's eastern regions. Located on the main thoroughfare are a telephone booth and a currency exchange office. Guatiza is, like Mala, a centre for the breeding of →*cochineal lice,* used in the production of carmesine pigment.

Other than the cactus fields, there is nothing much to see in Guatiza. The town lies within the administrative district of Teguise, the mayor of which had the neighbouring settlement of Los Cocoteros built in the hopes of attracting a wave of tourism. However, this complex never managed to achieve any significance as a centre for tourism. Today, it is predominantly the Spaniards who live here and no one seems concerned in the least with the maintenance of the dilapidated tourist complex.

Currency Exchange: Caja Insular de Ahorros, Ramirez Cerda s/n., Tel: 81 42 13.

Guest Houses →*Accommodation*

Haría

Haría is a green valley full of palm trees situated in the Barranco Tenesi canyon. Its relative abundance of water has brought this oasis modest prosperity. The surrounding regions otherwise comprise barren landscapes. A new ornithological park is presently in the planning stages; it is intended to make this area more attractive to visit.

The district of Haría has a population of around 15,000 with about 1,000 living in the city. To reach Haría, take the 2 kilometre (1½ mile) long road from Arrieta heading west.

When coming from Teguise, one need only to stay on the GC 730 northbound to get to Haría. Shortly before reaching the exit, the Mirador de Haría scenic overlook lies to the right of the road. From this vantage point, the fertile valley can be seen in its entirety. Also located here are a snack bar and a souvenir shop. After around 400 yards is a second scenic overlook before reaching Haría.

These scenic overlooks are Haría's main attraction. The view over the valley evokes images of relentless Arabian desert landscapes which only offer relief at an oasis.

Seen from closer up, the city in the "valley of a thousand palms" is only a town in which numerous palm trees grow. Haría has a certain arrogance about it due to its relative affluence; however, one will note that this is only a façade after a while. The farmers work here just as hard to make ends meet by selling their produce.

Tourism as a source of income does not play a significant role; it is only the Miradores, the scenic overlooks which attract tourists. The village itself with its winding alleyways and the activity can remind visitors of the work atmosphere at home so that Haría hardly profits at all from foreign tourism. Pub owners lock the doors to their toilets so that not every tourist travelling through uses their facilities without as much as drinking an espresso.

Haría / **Practical Information**

Accommodation: "Arrieta" Apartment House (one key), Caserio de Arrieta. Eight apartments priced between £14.50 and £18 ($25 and $32).

Restaurants: "Las Baleos" Bar/Restaurant, diagonally across from the plaza. The owner seems to expect only men as guests since the ladies' toilet is locked; the reason, as explained above.

"Puerta Oerde" Restaurant, across from the plaza with specialities from the grill.

"El Cortiga" Restaurant, an old farmhouse which was converted into a restaurant and serves Canarian cuisine at reasonable prices. When coming from the Mirador del Rio heading toward Teguise, the restaurant is located on the outskirts of Haría.

Important Addresses

City Hall/Tourist Information: Calvo Sotelo 1, Tel: 83 50 09.

Post Office: Calle Calvo Sotelo.

Currency Exchange: Caja Insular de Ahorros, Trece de Septiembre 1, Tel: 83 50 15.

Telephone: on the plaza in the centre of town.

Police: Carretera Local Orzola KM 0.800, Tel: 83 50 08; Calvo Sotelo 1, Tel: 83 50 09.

Taxis: Primo de Rivera, Tel: 83 50 31.

Health Insurance

It is recommended to take out a travel health insurance policy for the duration of the trip _(→Insurance)._

The Spanish physicians will charge directly for treatment. Upon returning home, invoices for medical treatment and medication must be presented to one's insurance company. For this reason, one should always ask for an invoice after visiting a clinic, hospital or doctor's office.

History

Lanceloto Malocello, an adventurer from Genoa Italy was the first to visit this island in 1312. The island's name was derived from Lanceloto. At least this is one theory. Others claim that the island was named after Lancelot, a companion of Jean de Bethancourt during his conquest of the island. Whichever is the case, Lanceloto Malocello experienced the island much more beautiful and fertile than it is now. The profile of Lanzarote today is the result of the volcanic eruptions around 450 years after Malocello's visit.

Lanceloto not only left behind his name for the island, but also the foundations of its oldest building. In the middle of the 14th century, he had a fortress built in honour of Saint Barbara on the Guanapay near the city of Teguise, later to become the capital of the island. The fortress suffered greatly under various invasions over the years, later to be rebuilt and expanded by a Spanish captain. In addition, the architect Leónardo Torriani added the final touches in 1596. The fortress was renamed and is still known today as Castillo de Guanapay. Up to 1402, no one – with the exception of Lanceloto Malocello – really took note of the island. It is possible that some African seafarers did come to the island on occasion to undertake some explorations. Or they might have come in search of the purple orchil lichen used in making purple dyes

Typical for Lanzarote: white houses against the contrasting black of the volcanic landscape

which consequently gave Fuerteventura and Lanzarote the name "Purpurarias" or the purple islands. What is considered certain is that the visitors took the local residents back and sold them as slaves in Africa and Europe. The Spanish knight Almonaster is nonetheless said to have set foot on the Lanzarotan coast in 1393. On his return, he brought several prisoners and fruits as evidence of the wealth of the entire archipelago.

The Norman Jean de Bethancourt took interest in the island in 1402. The Baron of Saint Martin de Gaillard in the dutchy of Eu in Normandy was King Charles VI's chamberlain after he had gained renowned as a seafarer and warrior. Bethancourt had just about had enough of serving in the royal court with a king who was close to insanity. And then he heard of Almonaster and the islands in the Atlantic. This was the opportunity to conquer something and add to his fame. On May 1, 1402, Bethancourt sailed out of the La Rochelle harbour accompanied by his deputy Gadifer de la Salle and the chaplains Juan de Verier and Pedro Bontier. The latter were not only men of the cloth but also charged with the duties of chroniclers. As with any conqueror, there were also soldiers on board and two interpreters who had been captured from the island during the previous year: Isabel and Fernando.

The travel route took the ship to Vivero, Coruña and Cadiz where around 26 men abruptly deserted. Fifty-six formed the core of the crew and saw the Isletas Alegranza, Montaña Clara and Graciosa followed by Lanzarote come into view. It was the month of July and eight day's journey from Cadiz.

The island was originally divided into two kingdoms which were then united under the mighty King Zonzomas. During his lifetime, a powerful storm swept the Basque Martin Ruiz de Avendaño to the island. Zonzomas was benevolent and let the shipwrecked crew stay in his palace and even offered the captain the services of his wife Fayna. Avendaño didn't have to be asked twice.

Fayna was not only beautiful but fertile as well and bore a daughter, Ico, only a short while thereafter. Ico would later become famous for her beauty. In addition, she was the daughter of a king and by no means impoverished. The successor to Zonzomas' throne was his son Tiguafaya, on which fortune was not to smile. The king and his wife were enslaved by pillaging Spaniards. With this, the throne was vacant, making way for a man by the name of Guanarame who was married to the beautiful Ico. Ico was considered illegitimate, which quite annoyed the island's populace. They demanded a trial by fire: the unfortunate Ico was sealed in a hot, smoky room with three contemptible women; the theory being, only a woman with noble blood could survive this trial. Ico took the advise of a wise elder and soaked a sponge in water and took it with her into the room. With this, she was able to survive the smoke.

Consequently, she was recognised as legitimate and her son Guadarfia, as the legitimate heir to the throne. Just then, the conquerors arrived.

When the natives saw the Normans land, the quickly retreated into the mountains. They still called their island "Titeroygatra" and served Guadarfia. Guadarfia was anything but a warrior. His island was plundered so often during his lifetime, that he simply had no more desire to get involved in battles. The invaders – and this was something quite new for Guadarfia – approached him in friendship. And since the invaders did not plan to kill him and his people, he even welcomed and helped them build the El Rubicon Fortress in the southwestern regions of the island. It was there that plans for the conquest of Fuerteventura were forged.

Juan de Bethancourt's accomplishment was not having spilled a drop of blood during this new conquest. He then returned to Spain. He stood in the service of the Castillian crown and now needed new men; after all, he hoped that the luck he had with Lanzarote would hold out in his conquests of the neighbouring island.

However, if the cat's away...: Gadifer de la Salle was an enthused sea lion hunter and the comical animals could be found on Lobos, the island between Lanzarote and Fuerteventura. While de la Salle hunted, the commander of the El Rubicon Fortress, Bertin Berneval, instigated an uprising and attacked Guadarfia. Berneval took several natives as slaves, loaded them on a ship and disappeared with them to Spain. Meanwhile, Gadifer de la Salle had almost died of thirst on Lobos: he had sent his friend Remonnet to Lanzarote by ship to get supplies. Berneval's men took the ship as well as the food and weapons which were stored in El Rubicon. If it weren't for the Spanish captain Francisco Calvo and his ship named "Morella", the Normans would have died of thirst or starved to death on Lobos. The two chaplains Bontier and Verier managed to convince Calvo to sail to Lobos and rescue de la Salle.

The native population was meanwhile appalled at these events which were Berneval's answer to their hospitality: they pulled out all the stops and attacked the Europeans killing some of them. The paltry rest barricaded themselves in the fortress near Arrecife.

Gadifer de la Salle, who managed to narrowly escape death once more, now planned to take over the island. The native Atchen, an ambitious young man who wanted to become king of Lanzarote suggested taking Guadarfia prisoner so he himself could take the throne. And indeed: numerous Guanches were taken prisoner; all were then freed, except one – the king.

However, Atchen actually wanted nothing to do with the Spanish conquerors and launched an attack on them. In the subsequent tumult, Guadarfia managed to escape and his vengeance was bitter. Atchen was burned alive. Guadarfia was enraged: he was king and his people mutinied? Not with him! The king fought with a group of his staunch allies with the intention of killing all of the natives with the exception of women and children. The two chaplains managed to prevent this. They quickened their pace in spreading their religion and baptised many, although some of these new converts then became slaves.

When Jean de Bethancourt returned to Lanzarote in the spring of 1404, only 300 of his men were still alive. Guadarfia defended himself no longer and surrendered on February 27 with his men. He was then baptised by Father Verier under the name Luis. He was subsequently set free and even given some land. For the priest, this was the first victory for Christianity in this part of the world.

From then on Jean de Bethancourt was underway between Spain and the islands of Lanzarote and Fuerteventura. He was even crowned king of the conquered island, administrated by his viceroy and nephew Maciot de Bethancourt. On December 13, 1406, Jean de Bethancourt invited everyone who had a problem with this decision to the El Rubicon fortress. Among his guests were the leader of the Guanches, and the native population. Bethancourt demanded that they obey the orders of Maciot and give him a fifth of their harvests. On December 15, Jean de Bethancourt set off to sea quite satisfied. It was reported that even the native population was rather sad to see their "generous" conqueror set sail.

From then on, Jean de Bethancourt determined his claims on territory with the pope and the Castillian crown and received reports on the events on his favourite island, Lanzarote, on a regular basis. However, he was never again to set foot on the island. He died in 1425 in his palace and was buried in Grainville la Teinturiere in the Normandy in the village church in front of the main altar.

Maciot de Bethancourt hurried to establish a capital city from which he would rule the island. Since he had meanwhile fathered children with one of King Guadarfia's daughters, he named this city after her: Teguise. Maciot's greed grew. He demanded his fifth of the populace's income unbendingly – and brought the residents to ruin. Finally, he had the natives of Lanzarote captured and – despite the fact that they had been baptised – had them sold as slaves in Europe.

When the bishop of San Marcial de Rubicon, Alberto de las Casas died, the fate of the tortured populace seemed to change course. Brother Mendo de Biezma took over the bishopric and attempted to halt Maciot in his activities of selling his subjects into slavery. The bishop's advice fell on deaf ears. The bishop then made the report of his tyrannic activities to the Spanish Queen Catalina. The queen could never tolerate tyrants and ordered Enrique de Guzman, Count of Niebla to take three battle ships under the command of Pedro Barba de Campos to the Canary Islands. Maciot smelled a rat, sold off the island which he had only administered for his uncle to Enrique of Portugal and set off for Madeira where he died in 1452.

Lanzarote then changed hands a number of times finally to land under Andalusian rule. When Jean de Bethancourt died, the island was owned by no one at first because his nephew was not his legitimate successor and heir, not to mention that his character was highly questionable. The island then went back to the Castillian crown. This caused an uprising in the Lanzarotan population. In the streets of Teguise, it came to bloody conflict between the Spaniards and the natives who were not willing to bow to the Spanish crown but on the other hand, they were not willing to be ruled by the ambitious members of the Herrera family who also staked territorial claims on Lanzarote. Ultimately, this family also mixed in with the conquering of the neighbouring islands. The bottom line: Lanzarote remained Castillian. Diego de Herrera was granted an enormous sum of money amounting to five million Maravedis in compensation and became Count of the Canary Island of La Gomera. Lanzarote remained under Spanish rule up until present.

Holiday Apartments →*Accommodation*

Holidays and Celebrations

General Holidays:
In addition to Maundy Thursday, Good Friday, Christmas Eve, Easter, Christ's Ascension, Pentecost and Corpus Christi;

January 1: New Year's Day

January 6: Epiphany, celebrated with presents for the children; parades and processions on all of the islands

February/March: "Carnival", the biggest, loudest and most colourful celebration on the archipelago, making this a travel destination for many Continental Europeans during this season

March 14: St. Joseph's Day

April 1: Day of Victory in the Civil War
May 1: Labour Day
May 30: Dia de Canarias
May/June: Corpus Christi, with huge carpets of flowers in La Oratova and La Laguna
June 29: Peter and Paul
July 18: Day commemorating the National Uprising
July 25: St. Jacob's Day (patron saint of Spain)
August 15: Mary's Ascension
October 12: Anniversary of the discovery of America ("Dia da Raza")
November 1: All Saint's Day
December 8: Immaculate Conception
December 25: Christmas Day
Holidays and Celebrations on Lanzarote:
May 24: Maria Auxiliadora Festival in Montaña Blanca near San Bartolomé;
June 13: San Juan Festival in Haría;
June 29: San Pedro Festival in Maguez;
July 7: San Marcial de Rubicon Festival, in honour of the island's patron saint in Femés.
July 16: Virgen del Carmen Festival in Teguise and Puerto del Carmen;
August 24: San Bartolomé Festival in San Bartolomé
August 25: Patron Saint Ginés Festival on the island;
September 15: Virgen de los Volcanos Festival in Tinajo;
October 7: Virgen del Rosario Festival in Arrecife;
November 30: San Andres Festival in Tao;
December 4: Santa Barbara Festival in Maguez;
December 8: official Inmaculada Concepción holiday;
December 24: Rancho de Pascua Festival in Teguise.

Insurance

Supplemental health insurance for the duration of one's stay on Lanzarote is recommended. Some insurance companies also offer a travel package with insurance coverage for everything from liability, to accidents, theft and lost luggage.

International Press

Newspapers in the English language are available in the larger cities and tourist centres of Lanzarote, Fuerteventura, Gran Canaria, Tenerife and La

Palma – this, however, with a delay of at least one day. Also among the selection are national and international magazines. On El Hierro and La Gomera, finding newspapers and magazines in English can be somewhat more difficult.

Newspapers and magazines can be purchased at the newsstands and in the "Librerías". There are also travel guides on the Canary Islands in these shops. On the larger islands, there are also magazines and newspapers produced especially for tourists, for instance "Canarias Tourist" or "Lanzarote". In these papers, tips and trends on the islands are covered as well as giving businesses the opportunity to advertise. These newspapers and magazines cost between 35p (60¢) and £3.50 ($4.25).

Lanzarote / International Press

One additional foreign language publication on Lanzarote is the island's news magazine "Lancelot" which is published in Spanish, English and German. The editorial staff of this magazine celebrated their sixth birthday on August 30, 1987 with 222 Spanish, 20 English and 13 German issues in print.

The magazine costs around £1.75 ($2) and is – in addition to being a medium for advertisers – a declaration of love to the volcanic island of Lanzarote. "Hot" topics covered include agriculture during the Franco era; day tours on Fuerteventura are also described in brief articles; and "Lancelot" also reports on current happenings on the island. Those interested in just what the artist César Manrique is doing at the moment will also find this covered in this magazine.

Isletas

The Isletas or small islands in Lanzarote's northern regions encompass a total area of a little under 40 square kilometres (16 square miles). The largest of these is →*Graciosa* with an area of 27 square kilometres (10 square miles), its highest elevation being the Pedro Barba reaching 266 metres (870 feet). Graciosa is accessible by ferry departing from →*Orzola.* The other Isletas, their areas and highest elevations are as follows:

Alegranza, 12 km^2 (4.7 sq. miles); La Caldera, 289 m (945 ft)
Montaña Clara, 1.1 km^2 (.43 sq. milles); Montaña Clara 256 m (837 ft)
Roque del Este, .07km^2 (.027 sq.miles); El Companario, 84 m (275 ft)
Roque del Oeste .06 km^2 (.023 sq. miles);El Roque: 41 m (134 ft)

Isleta → *La Isleta*
Islote de Hilario → *Montañas del Fuego*

Jameos del Agua

The largest lava cave on Lanzarote, Jameos del Agua, is not far from the Cueva de los Verdes and lies near Lanzarote's northeastern coast. Coming from Arrecife, keep to the right after Arrieta and turn right 4 (2½ miles) later. From Cueva de los Verdes, stay on the road to the coast which leads directly to Jameos del Agua.

Jameos is a word originating from the Arabic languages and is translated as "fireplace" or "chimney", referring here to the opening of an extensive system of caverns. Jameos del Agua marks the end of a 7 kilometre (4½ mile) natural tunnel left behind by cooling lava flows in the Malpaises de Corona. At least in its original state.

The successful union of architecture and landscape, in harmony with each other on the island of Lanzarote

What man has made out of this is a fascinating example of architecture in harmony with nature; the architect, →*César Manrique*. Not only people but birds feel at home in Jameos del Agua as well. There are flowers, huge cactuses and a pool designed by this architect and set off in white, a contrast to the surrounding landscapes. However, it may not be used by visitors to swim in. Thousands of tourists would otherwise take a dip within the sweeping curves of this swimming pool.

Not to worry, though, there is a lot more to see anyway during a visit to Jameos del Agua: the restaurant and bars serve coffee and cake in addition to hearty meals.

The prices are reasonable despite the fact that this grotto counts among the most enchanting attractions on Lanzarote.

Around eight metres (26 feet) below the "Manrique pool" lies a small lake, linked to the sea, explaining its high salt content. This natural pool is the habitat for small, blind, white crabs. These albinos are a phenomenon of nature said to be unique in all the world.

Along the lake are stone slab steps which also mark the beginning of the Jameos Night Club's dance floor. Swimming is not allowed in the grotto's lake. The grotto is open daily from 11 am to 6:45 pm. An admission of £3.75 ($6.25) is charged for this architectural masterpiece.

On Tuesdays, Fridays and Saturdays, Jameos del Agua is transformed into a discotheque from 7 pm to 3 am. Admission is around £6 ($10) which includes one drink.

Janubio

Janubio lies due north of Playa Blanca to the left of the main road. The salt flats shimmer in hues of white and pink.

In order to extract around 10,000 tons of salt annually, sea water is pumped into the salt flats. Today, this pumping process is powered by electricity; earlier, this was accomplished through the use of windmills. The wind then sweeps over the full pools for several weeks. After four weeks, the salt is removed by shovel and dried. Ice and the traditional sea salt are used by the fishing industry to preserve their catch. Only a small proportion of this salt is used as table salt.

La Asomada

La Asomada comprises around thirty houses and lies southeast of the Montañas del Fuego between the GC 730 and GC 720 roadways west of Tias.

A public telephone as well as a post box can be found along the main roadway. When coming from the Montañas del Fuego, one will see a house to the left with impressive cactuses. There are no restaurants in La Asomada.

La Caleta

In contrast to La Restingua, the old Canarian architecture has remained intact in La Caleta, a fishing village in Lanzarote's northern regions. The bays cut deep into the coastal cliffs and the white beach of Playa de Famara are the trademarks of La Caleta, the full name of which is La Caleta de Famara.

The promenade along the coast which consists of rough volcanic blocks has seen better days. Many of the glass panes have fallen out of the lanterns and tiles are missing from the promenade. This town seems unbearably deserted especially during the winter. The sea is so rough during this season that La Caleta can hardly attract anyone at all. The coast is considered an underwater paradise but the sea is often so rough that the red flag is hoisted on Playa de Famara on a regular basis, meaning that swimming is outright dangerous. The Playa de Famara beach is long with fine sand but not terribly attractive to look at since it is strewn with thorny bushes and scattered stones.

A captain misjudged the coastline here and promptly ran aground with his shipload of cement. The ship's hull broke in two. What remains of the ship, foremost the masts, juts out of the water as an unsightly pile of rubble – a foreboding sight. It is not at all a good idea to pay a visit to this shipwreck, especially during rough seas. This is not only extremely dangerous, it could prove fatal.

Somewhat inland toward Teguise, one will pass the Urbanización La Famara. A clever planner took up on the motif of Lanzarotan agriculture. Where otherwise plants grow in funnel-shaped hollows in the volcanic soil surrounded by small walls to provide protection from the wind, it is predominantly Dutch visitors who live in these round bungalows. However: the overall impression is somehow out of sync with itself. The idea seems plagiarised and misinterpreted; the settlement, anonymous and lifeless since all activity is shielded by the walls.

There is a shopping centre in the Urbanización and cars can also be rented here. Those wanting to eat out or seeking diversion will find they have to drive to La Caleta. The fish dishes served in the restaurants are especially tasty.

La Caleta / **Practical Information**
Accommodation
"Playa Famara" Apartments (two keys), Playa de Famara, Tel: 84 51 32, 146 bungalow apartments priced from £24 to £46 ($41 to $78).
Restaurants
"La Caleta" Restaurant.
"El Risco" Restaurant.
"Montaña Lina" Bar/Restaurant.
"Sol" Bar/Restaurant.
"Casa García" Restaurant.
Shopping: There is a shopping centre in the Urbanización Famara as well as two grocery stores in La Caleta.
Telephone: A telephone can be found in the "La Caleta" restaurant.

La Geria

The honeycombed landscape of La Geria, situated between Arrecife and the Montañas del Fuego is characteristic of Lanzarote. After the volcanic eruptions of the 18th and 19th centuries, a third of the island was blanketed in lava and volcanic ash. In addition, Lanzarote is an island on which rain is a relatively rare occurrence; some years it doesn't rain at all.

And still: the farmers do not despair. The volcanic lapilli layers absorb the scarce rainwater like a sponge and numerous plants take advantage of extracting the water from the volcanic rock with their roots. The fact that the stone also contains an abundance of minerals necessary for plant growth was more quickly recognised by the plants than by mankind. Prickly pears grow on a base of basalt and sand. A mixture of the two can even support watermelons.

The farmers took the initiative: if the soil was going to be stingy, then it was necessary to use it in the most efficient way possible. They dug funnel-shaped craters into the basalt lapilli soil composed of volcanic ash and planted grapevines, for example, at the centre of each. After this, they built retaining walls in the form of a semicircle to protect the plants from the wind. The plants did not wither and die and the fertile components of the soil present here were not eroded away by the wind.

Another agricultural method not only used in the La Geria region but on almost all of Lanzarote is to plant the plants in the fertile soil and cover this with a layer of porous lipilli several inches thick. For decades, the plant can then extract the necessary moisture and nutrients from the soil.

Especially attractive fields exemplary of this "en arenando" method of cultivation can be found between La Geria and the oasis town of →*Haría*. The most common crops are onions, sweet potatoes and prickly pears which thrive in this region.

The green plants in the earthen funnels make such a picturesque contrast to the dark volcanic soil that this region was immortalised in the catalogue for the Museum of Contemporary Art in New York as art with no artist – an example of landscape engineering with no engineer.

La Graciosa →*Graciosa*

La Isleta

La Isleta is a peninsula west of Costa Blanca in the northern regions of Lanzarote. Many refer to this area as "La Santa Sport" (Saint Sport) after the apartment complex located here (Tel: 84 01 00). The complex on this remote peninsula can accommodate 1,400, offering every type of sport imaginable. The 415 apartments range in price from £62 to £120 ($107 to $207) per night, including the use of all the sports and recreational facilities. However, only members of this time-sharing complex are allowed on the grounds. Over the years of spending their holidays here, these members gain equity in the complex.

Top sports personalities from all over the world train here. The public transportation is, however, so poor that the holiday visitors staying here remain almost exclusively within the complex. Even when everything imaginable is available within the complex, those staying in this club do seem isolated from the rest of Lanzarote and the rest of the world.

La Respingona

La Respingona marks a tragic chapter in tourism on the Canary Islands, having to do with real estate speculation. This town on Playa San Juan west of Playa de Famara and La Caleta consists of neglected, prefabricated houses. Paint can be seen peeling off the walls and window frames of these residential units. "Hollanza" is the name of this settlement built by an optimistic Dutch company which obviously expected more activity on Lanzarote's rugged northern coast.

The houses make for an unpleasantly sharp contrast to the landscape. This settlement has just as little to do with Canarian architecture as it does with César Manrique's philosophy of keeping architecture in harmony with nature.

Language

Although the official language on Tenerife is Spanish, the two other widely spoken languages are English and German. Many announcements are made in English and numerous waiters will be able to communicate in English. Being able to speak even a little Spanish will still be advantageous, not only as a courtesy. It is also quite fun to have a command of at least a little of this fiery, temperamental language – even if speaking slowly and stuttered.

The Canarians are thankful even if the visitor merely makes an effort to speak their language. In more remote towns, it is even a necessity to speak some Spanish, even if one points and has prices written down while shopping. Resourceful gestures or pantomiming are always helpful.

A small Spanish dictionary should definitely be brought along – if all else fails, one can always point to the appropriate word. The pronunciation of the Spanish language is relatively easy – and one will not have to learn a new alphabet as is the case with Greek.

The vowels a, e, i, o, and u are pronounced longer.

The consonants in alphabetical order:

b and v are pronounced somewhere between an English b and v;

c before an a, o or u is pronounced as a k;

c before e or i is the same as the hard English th as in thing;

ch is pronounced like the English ch, as in cheese;

d is pronounced like a quick ds and is only spoken very slightly at the end of a word;

f like f;

g before a, o or u is pronounced gutturally like the ch in the Scottish "Loch", for example "gente" = people;

gu or gue is pronounced as a hard g. War = guerra is pronounced gerra, not goo-era or with a guttural g;

gü, which is quite seldom in the Spanish language, indicates that a word is to be pronounced like gui or gue (gwi and gway), for example, a town on Lanzarote – Güime, will offer the chance to practice this;

h is a silent letter, horarios (time table) is pronounced orarios;

j is a gutturally pronounced h;

l like l;

ll like ly;

m like m;

n like n;

ñ like ny as in canyon or like the gn in cognac.

p is spoken much softer, almost like a b;
q like k;
r is rolled at the beginning of a word, otherwise it has the colouring of a d;
rr is definitely a rolled r as in "carretera", the motorway;
s is only hinted at the end of the word, otherwise it is slightly harder;
t like t;
v is pronounced like a b;
x is spoken more softly, more like a gs than a ks;
y in Spanish is either a) a vowel like an e or b) a consonant pronounced like the English y;
z pronounced like a soft th.

Phrases

Mister	Señor
Mrs.	Señora
Ladies and Gentlemen	Señoras y señores
Do you speak English/Spanish?	Habla usted ingles/español?
Yes, I speak... No, I don't speak...	Si, hablo... No, no hablo...
Yes, a little.	Si, un poco.
Good Morning! (until noon)	Buenos días.
Good Day/Evening! (until dusk)	Buenos tardes.
Good Night!	Buenos noches.
See you soon!	Hasta pronto! Hasta luego!
See you this evening!	Hasta la noche!
Good-bye!	Adios!
yesterday, today, tomorrow	ayer, hoy, mañana
How are you?	Como esta? or Que tal?
I am fine/not so good	Me va bien/mal.
I am not doing too well.	No me siento bien.
My name is ...	Mi nombre es ...
I would like ...	Tengo un deseo
why?	Por que?
what's wrong? what's up?	Que pasa?
Where is...?	Donde esta
the nearest post office?	la proxima oficina de correos?
the police station?	el puesto de policía
the hospital?	el hospital?
the pharmacy?	la farmacia

Yes, no	si, no
please	por favor
Yes, that's possible	si, es posible.
Thank you.	Gracias.
Excuse me!	Perdone!
No problem. Don't mention it.	No importa. De nada.
What time is it?	Que hora es?
I am hungry/thirsty.	Tengo hambre/sed.
I would like something to eat.	Quisiera/Me gustaria comer algo.
How much does this cost?	Cuanto cuesta esto?
What would you like?	Que desea Usted?
Do you have...?	Tiene Usted?
half a pound	media libra
kilogramme	kilo
a bottle of red/white wine	una botella de vino blanco/tinto

Numbers

0 = cero, 1 = uno/una, 2 = dos, 3 = tres, 4 = cuatro, 5 = cinco, 6 = seis, 7 = siete, 8 = ocho, 9 = nueve, 10 = diez, 11 = once, 12 = doce, 13 = trece, 14 = catorce, 15 = quince, 16 = dieciseis, 17 = diecisiete..., 20 = veinte, 21 = veintiuno/veintiuna, 22 = veintidos, 30 = treinta, 40 = cuarenta, 50 = cincuenta, 60 = sesenta, 70 = setenta, 80 = ochenta, 90 = noventa, 100 = ciento, 101 = ciento uno/ciento una, 200 = doscientos/-as, 1000 = mil.

Las Breñas

Around 8 kilometres (5 miles) north of Playa Blanca on the road to Arrecife, one will come to an intersection where the road to the left leads off to Janubio and El Golfo. The road to the right leads toward Las Breñas. One will pass flat, volcanic hills of black lava, fields framed in volcanic stone and snow white houses scattered in the landscape.

After 2 kilometres (1¼ mile), a roadway leads off to the right to Las Breñas. Among the approximately 40 houses belonging to the grain farmers are two grocery stores which are, however, not readily recognisable as such from the outside.

The Plaza de Victor Fernandez Gopar was laid out across from the plain San Luis Gonuage Church in 1987. The flowers have a refreshing effect amid the volcanic browns and the contrast of the white walls. Below the church are a playground and the town's bus stop.

Literature

Only one Canarian was to gain literary fame: Benito Perez Galdos (1843-1920). The theatre in Las Palmas de Gran Canaria was named in his honour. His series of novels "Episodios Nacionales" comprises 46 volumes. These are not recommended as holiday reading.

The first descriptions of the islands originate from the Italian engineer Leonardo Torriani (1590) and from Padre Espinosa (1595). The author Don Jose Viera y Clavio published three volumes in 1770: "Historia Generale de las Islas Canarias". These historical works have in part been translated into other languages (English and German). Further information is available in the book stores on the Canary Islands.

Lobo →*Geography*
Los Ajaches →*Geography*

Los Cocoteros

A roadway around 2 kilometres (1¼ miles) in length leads from Guatiza to the Urbanización Los Cocoteros. There is no infrastructure which could attract tourists to Los Cocoteros. However, it is a dreadful example of a residential area intended to ooze with harmony. Los Cocoteros cannot deny that it evolved on a drawing board. It includes a restaurant, a supermarket and the ceramics studio belonging to the artist José Jesus Brito. South of Los Cocoteros are a few old salt flats from which a handful of fishermen still do extract salt to preserve their catch.

Los Hervideros

The rugged coastline of Los Hervideros lies between the Salinas de Janubio and El Golfo in Lanzarote's western regions. The barren landscape is full of jagged volcanic rock and ash. Los Hervideros is a destination offered by numerous sightseeing buses but is also visited by those discovering the island on their own. In this barren landscape, the ocean's surf has eroded labyrinths into the lava flows – all that grows here are green lichens on volcanic rock.

The ocean shimmers along the coast, then pounds the coastal cliffs foaming white. "Hervideros" is the Spanish word for sea foam.

Shortly before reaching the Salinas, one will find a grotto which falls off sharply to the sea. This beautiful scene is not easily captured on film since hiking down the rocks is more like sliding down the rocks. Only those with sturdy shoes should risk this hike. A rope is almost necessary to climb back up to the top. The light green volcanic "olivina", also called peridot, is sold along the coast of Los Hervideros. The colour of this semi-precious stone results from magnesium and iron silicates which formed millions of years ago. There are only a handful of volcanic islands on which olivina can be found; this stone is exported to Tenerife among other destinations. The demand for this stone has always been high since it is similar in appearance to emeralds. During the Baroque period, it was used to embellish churches.

Lucha Canaria

The Canarian form of wrestling has become the most popular sport on the islands – a sport which unique to the Canaries. Lucha is more than a simple wrestling match by which a lot of dust is churned up. It is a sport with set rules and tradition, whereby a fair fight is emphasised, using all of the strength that a team can muster.

Two opposing teams confront each other, usually in an arena with a sand floor. Each team consists of twelve men, dressed in shirts and trousers which are rolled up above the calf. Within two minutes, the *luchadores* try to force their opponents to the ground fighting individually. The team which has touched the ground twice with a part of their body other than the feet has lost.

The wrestlers pant, stomp and shove their opponent back and forth. Those who can, will try to trick their opponents. Experienced fighters know that the opponents shove only to provoke being shoved and then quickly dodge the shove, hoping that the opponent will lunge into emptiness, falling to the ground. The wrestlers bow low to the ground, trying to catch the others by the trousers. This is an advantage: then it is quite easy to pull the opponents legs out from under him in an opportune moment. The origin of this type of wrestling is not known today. There are historians, who place the origin in ancient Egypt – and there was contact between Egypt and the Canary Islands thousands of years ago. What is certain is that this type of wrestling does not originate from Switzerland, although there is an alpine type of wrestling which is similar to Lucha Canarias.

This type of competitive sport takes place regularly on the Canary Islands. For information on these matches, one should pay attention to posters or ask at the hotel reception.

Macher

Only a few scattered houses make up the village of Macher between Tias and Uga. A delightful experience is a visit to the "Las Vegas" wine cellars. The wine cellars are accessible as follows: 3 kilometres (2 miles) beyond Tias, shortly before Macher, head toward Geria and Asomada to the next intersection (around 3 kilometres/2 miles). From there, turn left toward Yaiza and continue 300 to 500 yards on the GC 730. One will find the wine cellars on the right-hand side of the road. The two German shepherds are usually leashed. The grapes for the wine sold here grow in the "craters" in the →*La Geria* region. Each individual plant is tended separately. The resulting wines are delicious – especially the red wines. Dry wines can be purchased for around £1.80 ($3) per bottle and a liqueur wine very similar to sherry for around £2.50 ($4.25). **Car Rental:** Autos Cabrera Medina, Carretera Puerto del Carmen/Reina Sofia 18, Tel: 82 58 29.

Maguez

The small village of Maguez lies halfway between the scenic overlooks Mirador de Haría and Mirador del Rio. Maguez has a small church and the "El Trebol" Bar. The residents make their living from farming.
Those who wish to continue from Maguez to Mirador del Rio must pay very close attention. The signs are posted illogically in that they cannot be read when coming from this direction. One will reach the Mirador after about 6 kilometres (4 miles); one can turn off both before and after Ye.

Mala

Mala lies between Tahiche and Jameos del Agua. The town lives by raising maize (corn), onions, beets and especially from raising the cochineal lice (→*Economy*, →*Cochenille*, *Vegetation*). When approaching from the north, one will already see the church on the right-hand side of the main road. When coming from Guatiza to the south, one will pass by a windmill before reaching

Mala. One can enjoy a meal either in the "Pabellon" Restaurant or in the "Tunera" – there is a sign for the "Tunera" at the southern entrance to town. The Tunera is a destination for nudists. Nudism is normally prohibited in Spain, but this complex is so remote that nudists do not interfere with public order. A rugged 7 kilometre (4½ mile) trail leads to the camp and "Tunera" Restaurant. There are sports and recreational facilities as well as a supermarket among these bungalows. A natural swimming pool allows for swimming even when the seas are rough.

Malpais de la Corona

The Malpais de la Corona, the badlands at the base of the Corona, extend over 18 square kilometres (7 square miles) in Lanzarote's north from Arrieta to Orzola. The most famous attractions in this barren region are the caves Jameos del Agua and the Cueva de los Verdes.

The volcanic cone of Monte Corona formed quite near the Famara cliffs near La Caleta 3,000 years ago, south of where the village of Ye is located today. This volcano spewed molten lava over this region a number of times. Lava flows continued toward Famara down the 400 metre (1,300 foot) cliff and toward El Rio/Graciosa. This northern region is also called Guatifay or Famara Guatifay. Lava from the Corona then covered the northeastern regions of the island with a stream of lava reaching temperatures up to 1,000°C (1832°F) and volcanic ash. The lava flowed out 3 kilometres (2 miles) into the sea, increasing Lanzarote's land area by 24 square kilometres (9 square miles).

The volcano's crater, the origin of these changes, is 190 metres (622 feet) deep; the mountain reaches a height of 215 metres (818 feet). At its summit, it has a diameter of 450 metres (1,472 feet).

Several hundred volcanoes can be found on Lanzarote. Of them, Monte Corona is the most interesting also in terms of tourism. Geologically speaking, it is unique. The Corona spewed its lava predominantly to the east. The lava flows formed layers, turning petrified, then molten, fusing with other layers and creating subterranean corridors which became famous throughout the world as gallerias. While the surface cooled relatively quickly, lava continued to flow under the crust. A pipeline of sorts developed, the length of which is around 6,100 metres (almost four miles).

Gases then formed in this corridor and exploded, causing the roof to collapse. Other segments collapsed under their own weight, leaving behind bizarre exits called Jameos. Around 20 of these can be found in the Malpais de la Corona. Grottoes also formed in this corridor, as did the underground lake, the habitat of the blind, albino crabs. Water seeped through from the surface to collect in depressions left behind from the lava flow.

The volcanic tunnel on Lanzarote remains the largest of its kind in the world.

Mancha Blanca →*Tinajo*
Manrique →*César Manrique*

Maps

Maps are available free of charge from most of the car rental agencies, usually included in a wallet along with the registration papers. Normally, this is only a rough sketch on which only the main roads are included.

The "Tourist Map – Gran Canaria – Fuerteventura and Lanzarote" costs £1.50 ($2.65) and has a scale of 1:150,000 which sufficiently covers Lanzarote. The legend is also in several languages. On the back of the map, there are entries regarding the sights on these three islands.

Also with a scale of 1:150,000 is the "hymsa" map (1987, Madrid and Barcelona) for Gran Canaria which includes the islands of Fuerteventura and Lanzarote as well. This map cost around £1.35 ($2.35) on the islands. On the back of the city maps of the capitals of the three islands in this province: Las Palmas de Gran Canaria (more detailed), Arrecife and Puerto del Rosario (practically useless).

The "Hildebrandt" holiday map is available for £2.50 ($4.40) also with the islands of Lanzarote, Fuerteventura and Gran Canaria. Lanzarote is depicted in a scale of 1:190,000. The map includes distance tables and brief travel suggestions in English, German and French. For Lanzarote, this map is somewhat confusing due to the colours used.

The touring map "Lanzarote" published by Edición A. Murillo (Madrid, 1987) costs around £1.10 ($1.90). This map also lists the most significant attractions and included pictures. The scale of 1:100,000 provides a good overview of the island with a clearly understandable legend. In addition, all of the roads as well as hiking trails are included on this map.

Medical Care

Medical care on Lanzarote is satisfactory. In the larger cities and tourist centres, there are emergency centres, medical specialists and governmental or private clinics. In the smaller cities and villages, if one does not find a hospital then there will always at least be a Red Cross station. "Cruz Roja" is the Spanish term for these stations, which will at the very least be equipped with an ambulance. Red Cross employees can be recognised by a uniform similar to that of a soldier: a green battle uniform with laced black boots. One will also see them on the ferries operating between the islands. The following is a summary of the emergency medical services offered. Additional addresses and telephone numbers can be found under individual entries.

Arrecife

Spanish Red Cross (Cruz Roja), Tel: 81 20 62.

Hospital Insular, Juan de Quesada 37, Tel: 81 05 00.

Emergency Ward in the hospital, Tel: 81 22 50, 81 22 54 and 81 22 58.

Doctor Marin, Avenida Fred Olsen, Tel: 81 11 38 and 81 11 86.

Puerto del Carmen

British Scandinavian Clinic, Avenida de las Playas, on-call 24 hours.

"San Antonio" Emergency Clinic, Carretera Las Playas (Tias), Tel: 82 59 11.

→*Hospitals, Pharmacies, Health Insurance*

Medication

Some visitors will find that they react sensitively to the unaccustomed climate and food. The "Canarian fever" has quite often been the cause for spending a day in close proximity to certain facilities. In the tourist centres, there are always →*Pharmacies* which have meanwhile adapted to this tourist-specific problem. Charcoal tablets or laxatives for the opposite problem should be brought along. Foot powder will prevent foot fungus. The beaches are not always clean, which is also true for swimming pools and showers. Bandages for minor injuries and iodine will protect against infection, should one be injured on the stones at the beach. The Canary Islands – with the exception of Fuerteventura and Lanzarote – are a veritable paradise for hikers. The paths are, however, quite often slippery and rugged. Elastic bandages will help in case of sprains. Eye drops will be of help to those whose eyes react sensitively to the intense sunlight – especially on the beach. Suntan lotion should also be included in the suitcase. The skin must gradually become accustomed to the sun. Those who ambitiously try to tan quickly will find that the tan peels off just as quickly. The amount of exposure to the sun should be increased very gradually. It is also better to move about in the fresh air than to lie flat on the beach, where the sun is even more intense than inland due to the reflection of the water. →*Medical Care, Vaccinations, Equipment*

Mirador de Haría →*Haría*

Mirador del Rio

This scenic overlook, high above the El Rio strait which separates the island of Graciosa from Lanzarote's northern coast, is a work of art by →*César Manrique*. It is reminiscent of cave dwellings in which the original inhabitants of this island once lived. The Mirador is open daily from 11 am to 6:45 pm; admission is around £1.85 ($3.25). It is well worth the price even though this is not apparent by the outward appearance of the restaurant as seen from the parking area.

Hidden by this façade is an extensive, two-storey building with tastefully designed hallways, elegant sweeping staircases and rooms where one can take in this fascinating architectural feat over a meal. The view from the semi-circular window extends over the Salinas del Rio to the island of Graciosa which is accessible by ferry from Orzola.

From this restaurant's veranda, one looks down almost vertically to the flatlands extending to Punta de Fariones. During clear weather, the other Isletas can also be seen: Alegranza, Montaña Clara, Roque del Este and Roque del Oeste.

Money

There are no limits to the amount of foreign currencies allowed to be brought into the country; however, larger amounts which are subsequently bought to the Spanish mainland must be declared upon arrival. Spanish pesetas may also be brought into Spain in unlimited amounts. Per person, 100,000 pesetas and foreign currencies with a value of up to 500,000 may be taken out without having any questions asked.

Banks are open Monday to Friday from 9 am to 2 pm; on Saturdays to 1 pm. In addition, there are currency exchange offices ("Cambio") and money can also be exchanged at the reception of larger hotels – albeit at a less favourable exchange rate. The official exchange rates are posted in the banks. One can also ask for these in larger hotels.

Eurocheques are accepted. These have the advantage that the amount is not already deducted from a bank account before departing as is the case with traveller's cheques. However, traveller's checks are insured for the entire amount if lost or stolen. In Spain, the fees for cashing Eurocheques are lower than for traveller's cheques.

Montaña Clara →_Geography, Isletas_

Montañas del Fuego

The "mountains of fire" comprise a bizarre landscape north of El Golfo. Most of the volcanoes formed during the eruptions from 1730 to 1736. One-forth of Lanzarote's surface area (200 square kilometres/78 square miles) was blanketed in lava and ash at that time. The epicentre of volcanic activity lay in the Timanfaya area, another name for the Montañas del Fuego (→_Geography_ and _Parque Nacional de Timanfaya_).

If driving from Yaiza heading north, one will reach the entrance to the Montañas del Fuego area after around 7 kilometres (4½ miles). There is a little devil on signposts as a symbol marking the way. At the sign at the intersection, one must then turn left and brake rather abruptly. This is where an admission of £3.75 ($6.25) is charged for Spain's most fascinating rock pile.

The roadway leads farther through barren fields of ash, supporting only lichens and mosses to the parking area with the "El Diablo" Restaurant (open 9 am to 5 pm, Tel: 81 10 60 and 84 00 57). Here, guests are served steaks prepared over what is probably the world's only volcanic grill, reaching temperatures of up to 400°C (750°F). Those expecting to see bubbling molten rock under the grill's grate will be disappointed. However, the earth in the depression to the right of the hotel is still so hot that straw bursts into flame on contact. Guides often turn this into a more entertaining phenomenon by pouring water down metal pipes which then spews back out only a few seconds later, much like a geyser.

Prices are average in the "El Diablo" Restaurant. Those who wish to see the mountains of fire either before or after eating will have the opportunity to do so from the "El Diablo" Restaurant. Every hour, a bus takes passengers through this geologically unique volcanic landscape. The buses are free of charge. This is the only permitted option of encountering the Montañas del Fuego other than on the back of a dromedary (→_Parque Nacional de Timanfaya_). The tight schedule which this bus follows may be an annoyance to some; however, this helps protect the national park in its delicate balance from hordes of tourists. The drawback remains that one might not have as much time to take pictures or enjoy the scenery as one might like.

Monumento al Campesino

The Monumento al Campesino was erected by →*César Manrique* and his team between Mozaga and San Bartolomé in the centre of Lanzarote. This is a macro-sculpture in honour of the strong, hard-working farmers of this island. Somewhat odd, this monument is composed of cisterns formerly used on sailing vessels and it can be seen from quite a distance; at night, the monument is illuminated. With this monument, the artists established the link between the Atlantic and the scarcity of water which farmers, or *Campesinos* must deal with. Those who take a closer look will recognise a number of figures: in addition to the farmer and the dog are also animals traditionally used in farming – the dromedary and donkey. Those who don't understand this at first should look around Canarian farms: the monument is by no means out of context. Directly adjacent is a simple yet harmonically conceived farmyard, considered exemplary of Lanzarotan architecture. Here, farming equipment can also be seen. A restaurant and a bar with typically Canarian dishes and the locally produced malvasia (malmsey) wines can be found here as well.

A ceramics exhibit displays works by the artist Juan Jesus Brito, who painted a portrait of a royal Canarian family based only on historical documentation. However, the family does look like a group of dwarves and one needs a royal portion of humour to envision a king and his attendants.

Mozaga

The two roads from Teguise to Uga and Tinajo to Arrecife intersect in Mozaga.The Monumento al Campesino on the road to San Bartolomé built by César Manrique is a popular attraction in the Mozaga region. The town itself comprises only a handful of houses.

When coming from San Bartolomé, one will find the Bodega wine cellars where it is possible to purchase wine directly from the vinter.

Munique

Munique is a village along the road between Tiagua and Soo. The residents live predominantly by farming. Crops harvested in this region include grains, onions and potatoes.

Naos → *Arrecife*
National Park → *Parque Nacional de Timanfaya*

Nazaret

Those driving from Arrecife to Teguise will pass through Nazaret after 9 kilometres (5½ miles). Nazaret's prosperity is readily apparent.
The villas on the slopes of Montaña Ubique rarely belong to the farmers who work the fields in this area. This settlement belongs to Nazaret and is called Oasis de Nazaret. The residents here come from Arrecife or earn their living in the tourist centres.

Nudism

Among the local residents of the Canary Islands, nudism is frowned upon. They dress conservatively and also behave as such in public. Still, the Canarians do tolerate it on most beaches when women swim or sunbathe topless – and this at any age. Therefore, it is left up to the individual traveller how much skin he or she wishes to expose to the intensive rays of the sun. There is, however, a limit to this general rule: on Lanzarote, people go naked into restaurants, shops and bars just as seldom as in other countries. On the beaches, complete nudity is generally not acceptable, and this applies to men as well as women. There are, however, unofficial exceptions On Lanzarote, one of these is →*Mala*. There is a nudist colony along the coast near this town which is an entire holiday complex. Since there are no private beaches in Spain, it is possible to swim and sunbathe nude here after having conquered the strenuous trek to this beach. It requires a hike of a few kilometres through rugged terrain. Lanzarote's long beaches always offer the opportunity to find a secluded area or an isolated bay. The more secluded the area, the more "less" is possible. One should, however, respect the Spaniards sense of modesty and not be more outgoing than the Spaniards themselves – and by no means in their presence. Officially, bathing nude or even topless is prohibited.

Orzola

Orzola lies to the north of the Jameos del Agua grotto. This is the northernmost village on Lanzarote; residents make their living by fishing and earlier, by operating salinas (salt flats). The quickest way to reach Orzola is via the coastal road from Arrecife.

One will travel through an area with sand dunes to both side of the roadway. There are a few narrow trails leading into the terrain. On weekdays, this area is rather quiet. There is a small beach, Playa de Canteria, where swimming is permitted. The beach is white, meanwhile readily accessible and cleaned on a regular basis. Orzola is such a popular destination today that a visit on a Sunday or holiday is not recommended since parking capacity is exhausted. The Malpaises de Corona (Malpaises = badlands) are definitely worth a stop: the bizarre lava formations provide an impression of what force was set loose when the volcanoes erupted on Lanzarote during the 18th century.

Along the coast of Orzola are miocene limestone deposits with petrified ostrich eggs and land snails. Miocene is the second oldest period in the tertiary era. If driving toward the harbour, one will find a post box and a public telephone on the opposite side of the street next to a street lamp.

→*Graciosa* is considered an island for gourmets; it is accessible by ferry departing from Orzola's harbour. The "Maria del Pino" ferry departs for the neighbouring island of Graciosa daily at 10 am and 5 pm. The return ferry leaves from Caleta de Sabo on Graciosa for Orzola at 8 am and 4 pm.

On Graciosa, the means of transportation are dromedaries or simply walking.

Orzola / **Practical Information**

Accommodation

"Los Vientos" (The Winds) with four apartments. For other accommodations ask in the bar-restaurantes.

Restaurants

"Punta Fariones" Bar-Restaurant, serving fresh fish daily based on the morning's catch. Prices depend on the weight of the fish. Served with the fish are "papas arrugadas", the Canarian shrunken potatoes or french fries with mojo sauce. This restaurant is heavily frequented during the time before the ferry to Graciosa departs.

Additional Bar-Restaurants:

"Rebozo", across from the mole on the eastern side of the harbour is planned to be closed soon.

"El Callao" and "Alegranzu".

"Los Roques" on the main street serves fresh prawns as their house speciality.

Parque Nacional de Timanfaya

The Parque Nacional de Timanfaya is the only national park on Lanzarote. This relatively young volcanic landscape is composed of extensive lava fields and areas blanketed in volcanic ash covering an area of 5,107 hectares (12,786 acres).

This barren region is poor in plant and animal life. Due to its uniqueness as a volcanic landscape and the attraction it holds for the tourist industry, it was declared a nature reserve. Admission is around £3.75 ($6.25).

The mountains of fire *(→Montañas del Fuego)* are part of this national park. When coming from Yaiza, keep heading north and after about 3 kilometres (2 miles), one will pass by a parking area where not only cars and buses are parked, but dromedaries as well. There is a mineralogical museum to the right of this parking area which is built into the ground, making it difficult to spot at first glance. On display here is a collection of various mineralogical exhibits; the museum is open Monday to Friday from 8:30 am to 4 pm, no admission is charged. The one drawback is that the stones are not labelled with descriptions.

From here, one can only enter the volcanic terrain by taking a dromedary ride. Driving a car or hiking into the landscape from this parking area is prohibited. This rule is in part to ensure that the Africans who rent out dromedaries can make a living but also to hinder unchecked masses of tourists from ruining this delicate landscape.

A dromedary excursion costs around £6.25 ($10.50) for two people seated to the left and right of the animal's hump. Children are usually free of charge, but the keepers determine a price not based on age but on the child's size and weight.

When the caravan's capacity is full, then one is taken on a ten-minute tour through a lunar landscape comprising over 300 craters. In 1824, forty of these erupted simultaneously, burying ten towns.

The excursion does not go to the "Islote de Hilario" Restaurant. To get there, one must continue north from the parking area and then turn left into the Montañas del Fuego.

Peña del Chache *→Geography*

Pharmacies

Pharmacies ("farmacias") display a green or red Maltese cross. Those who have brought along a specific medication that cannot be purchased on Lanzarote should present the slip included in the packaging. This way, the pharmacist can at least identify a similar medication. Pharmacies on Lanzarote are generally well stocked. When purchasing prescription medication, one should request a receipt so that one is reimbursed by one's health insurance company upon returning home.

Photography

The same film and supplies are available on Lanzarote as are common in other western countries. This is especially true in the larger cities and holiday centres. Prices are also comparable. Comparison between prices at different stores can help save money. Film can be developed on the Canary Islands. One day or even one-hour developing service is available almost everywhere. The quality is generally good.

Visitors who would rather have their film developed at home need not worry about the x-rays during security checks at the airports. Baggage is x-rayed, but this will not damage the film. Those who have reservations about film with a light sensitivity over 1000 ASA can request that the security officials check through the baggage by hand.

It is always a question of tact when taking pictures of the local people. It can never hurt to ask courteously.

Playa Blanca

The port city and tourist centre of Playa Blanca lies around 40 kilometres (25 miles) from Arrecife at Lanzarote's southern extremes. The town is accessible via a well maintained road from Arrecife running through Tias, Uga and Yaiza. Playa Blanca can also be reached by bus from Arrecife in a little less than 1 hour. The beaches Playa de los Coloradas and Playa Mujeres, better known as the Papagayo beaches, lie to the east of Playa Blanca. There are four adjacent bays well suited to swimming and measuring 100 to 200 yards in length with fine, yellowish sand. The street through town leads by the ruins of the →*Castillo de las Coloradas* right on the tip of Punta del Aguila and near the old salinas (salt flats) similar to those near →*Janubio*. A small gravel beach can also be found here, offering more seclusion than the Papagayo beaches.

If one drives around the Punta de Papagayo, one will come upon Caleta Cognito and Caleta Larga which are also widely known for their fine-grained sand.

Within the town itself, one will find a number of bars and restaurants in addition to two large shopping centres on the harbour and in the centre of town. There are also various bazaars and souvenir shops near the plain, towerless Nuestra Señora del Carmen Church.

This also implies the course Playa Blanca's development will likely take. It is still a quaint town; however, to the east and west of town surrounding the harbour, huge hotel complexes are being built almost overnight. Aome of these buildings (→*Playa Blanca / Accommodation*) are, however, not lacking in architectural vision. Fortresses and gigantic palaces served as prototypes. The ferry to Fuerteventura departs from this harbour. For more information on excursions with the "Alisur" ferry to the neighbouring island of Fuerteventura →*Travel on Lanzarote*. Also situated here along the harbour is a 150 metre (490 foot) sand beach.

Deep-sea fishing excursions depart from here on the "Gladius" yacht, lasting from 9 am to 4 pm (Tel: 82 62 23 and 82 57 37). The active fishermen among the passengers pay around £37 ($63); spectators, £23 ($40). Half-day trips from 9 am to 1 pm and 1 to 5 pm are offered for £14 ($24). There is a 50% discount for children.

Playa Blanca / **Practical Information**

Accommodation

"Lanzarote Princess" Hotel (****), double rooms without breakfast are priced from £58 ($100).

"Lanzarote Park", 500 beds, Playa Blanca, Tel: 83 01 55.

Apartment House near the Nuestra Señora del Carmen Church with apartments priced from £37 ($63).

Hostal/Residencia "Playa Blanca" (**), Playa Blanca, Tel: 83 00 46. 11 rooms priced from £15 ($25).

Hostal/Residencia "Playa del Sol" (**), 10 rooms priced from £15 ($25).

"Casa del Sol" Apartment House (three keys), Urbanización Montaña Rosa, Playa Blanca. 63 apartments priced from £30 to £55 ($50 to $94).

"Las Casitas" Apartment House (three keys), Playa Blanca. 46 apartments priced from £30 ($50).

Car Rental

Auto Cabrera, Rent-A-Car Skandia, Autos Faycan (at the harbour).

Medical Care
The polyclinic across from the "Las Lapas" Hostal Residencia is open 24 hours.

Taxis
There is a taxi stand at the playground next to the bus stop and the car rental offices.

Playa de Famara →*La Caleta*

Playa de Janubio

The beach near the Salinas de Janubio measures approximately 300 metres (980 feet) in length with fine, black sand. This beach is accessible from Playa Blanca by taking a trail through the fields shortly before reaching the salt flats. There are neither toilets nor showers, merely a rubbish container. The surf is not very rough, making this an optimal area for novice surfers. Surfboards must be brought along.

Playa de la Garita

The Playa de la Garita beach lies south of the fishing village of Arrieta on Lanzarote's eastern coast. The beach measures around 400 metres (1,310 feet) in length and is stony. The water here is consistently warm; the sea, calm. Parking is available.

Playa Honda

Playa Honda is situated southwest of Arrecife, directly next to the island's airport. A lovely promenade along the sandy beach, lovingly maintained houses and good restaurants count among the attractions this settlement has to offer.

Playa Honda / **Practical Information**
Restaurants: "Playa Honda" Restaurant, Calle Princesa Ico, Tel: 84 41 73. Shrimps in garlic sauce is priced around £3.75 ($6.25); fish dishes from £3.75 ($6.25); gofio, enough for two people, £3.30 ($5.75); mixed salads from £2.20 ($3.75). The food is inexpensive and good.
Taxi and Telephone: at the end of the promenade on the corner of Calle Princesa Ico.

Police

There are three types of police in Spain and also on the Canary Islands: the "Policia Municipal" (dark brown uniforms) has the function to maintain order and is concerned mainly with traffic violations. The "Guardia Civil" (green uniforms) is responsible for emergencies, for instance when reporting a theft. The emergency telephone numbers are posted at every public telephone. The hotel reception will be able to help if there is a problem with the language. Remaining to be mentioned is the "General de Policia" which is responsible for felonies.

Politics

Politically speaking, this archipelago has been a part of Spain since being conquered in the 15th century. Today, the administration is divided into two Provinces; Las Palmas de Gran Canaria with Las Palmas de Gran Canaria as its capital is composed of the islands of Gran Canaria, Fuerteventura, Lanzarote and the Isletas (→*Geography*).

Santa Cruz de Tenerife is the second province with Santa Cruz de Tenerife as its capital and including the islands of Tenerife, La Palma, El Hierro and La Gomera.

On each of the islands, there is a "Cabildos Insulares" the independent insular administration.

In recent decades, the Canary Islands have witnessed the development of political groups who call for the independence of the archipelago. This is more or less an academic discussion; it is not likely that Spain will give up the control of these islands.

Population and People

The total population of the Canary Islands is estimated at 1.5 million to date. In 1980, 50,000 lived on Lanzarote; 19,000 on Fuerteventura; 630,000 on Gran Canaria; 610,000 on Tenerife, 24,000 on La Gomera, 6,000 on El Hierro and 81,000 on La Palma.

The number of tourists outnumbers that of the residents by far, which has a notable effect on the water supply (→*Water*).

Each island has its own character and is thus heavily influenced by its residents.

Lanzarote is – despite the volcanic mountains – flat, hot, the landscape formed by hard-working farmers and architects. The fields always appear well tended due to a special method of farming (→*Economy*). The residents live mainly from agriculture. Tourism remains limited to only a few areas.

Fuerteventura is for fishermen; agriculture has been neglected and has missed the opportunity of which for instance Lanzarote has taken advantage. The island is untamed, rugged and has long sandy beaches along its coastline, which attract visitors from all over the world.

Gran Canaria has the entire spectrum of landscapes: mountains, beaches and forests. The island is just as suited to agriculture as it is to fishermen and shepherds – and tourists. The same is true for **Tenerife.** Both of these, the largest islands of the Canaries, have absorbed the flood of tourism without losing their own character.

La Palma has only begun to become accustomed to the numerous visitors. When the international airport was opened in 1987, protest arose, directed toward the tourists who would now start to arrive. However, tourism would bring money – and foreigners were already there: the selling out of the island had begun much earlier. Many landowners do not even make the effort to find

Artistic yet still unpretentious: decorative wooden balconies are characteristic of the Canary Islands

Spanish buyers for their land. On signs posted in fields showing the owner's willingness to sell, "for sale" or "zu verkaufen" takes the place of "se vende". For this as well as other reasons, especially older residents fear being overrun. **El Hierro** and **La Gomera** are the most untamed, untouched and demanding of the Canary Islands. Those visiting these islands will have to adapt to the cold as well as the heat, to high as well as low humidity – and this separated only by a few miles. On La Gomera, it is only the Valle Gran Rey, the valley of the great kings, which has suffered from tourism. That which began as an alternative to the tourist centres is now leading to a questionable counter-culture with which only the most thick-skinned and entrepreneurial Canarians can cope: the prices are hardly any longer acceptable for the residents because in the past years, they have doubled or even tripled. Without respect for the natives, tourists swim naked and smoke questionable substances – quite unpleasant for the conservative residents. An assimilation or even an understanding between the young travellers and the residents of Valle Gran

Only after the intense heat of midday has subsided do the residents of Lanzarote go back outside to sit in front of their houses

Rey has not taken place. The visitors have brought with them a culture which they were not able to realise in their own country – and force it on their hosts. The inhabitants of the Canary Islands are hospitable as were their ancestors the Guanches. And of them, it is also said that they were hard-working, honest and enjoyed music, dancing and life. They met the challenge set forth by their environment which was often hostile. And so it remains today.

Postal System

Post offices are open Monday to Friday from 9 am to 1 pm and some reopen from 5 to 7 pm. Postage stamps can also be purchased in the "estancos", the tobacco shops, and at many of the hotel reception desks. They can also be purchased when buying postcards.

Letters of up to 20 grams and postcards sent to EC member states 45 Pesetas; to other countries within Europe, these cost 55 Pesetas. There is no extra fee for airmail delivery within Europe. Those who would like to have letters, parcels or money sent to them can do this by general delivery: "en lista de correos". One must ask for the exact address of the post office.

Post boxes for normal deliveries are yellow with two horizontal red stripes. The ones for express deliveries are red.

Prices →*Shopping*

Puerto del Carmen

The flat Playa de los Picollos beach begins in the district of Playa Blanca (not to be confused with the town of Playa Blanca) in the former fishing town of Puerto del Carmen southeast of Arrecife. Today, Puerto del Carmen is one of the most important tourist centres on Lanzarote alongside Costa Teguise, Arrecife and the town of Playa Blanca. Puerto del Carmen consists of hotels, bars, discotheques and beaches with fine, light-coloured sand. Hardly anything remains of the quaint atmosphere of the former fishing village. Instead, small shops, boutiques, souvenir shops, restaurants, cafés and bars line the coastal street. The beach falls off gently into the sea, making it appropriate for children.

Although the tourist infrastructure is concentrated here like nowhere else on the island with the possible exception of Costa Teguise, Puerto del Carmen has still not reached the extremes of tourism present in Maspalomas on Gran Canaria for example. Puerto del Carmen extends for miles along the coast without going far at all inland. There are still only a few multi-storey buildings and actually only one beach which is very popular in the district of Playa Blanca.

Puerto del Carmen / **Practical Information**

Accommodation

"Los Fariones" Hotel (****) Puerto del Carmen, Tel: 82 51 75. 325 rooms with a view of the sea and private terraces. Tennis courts, miniature golf, tropical gardens and direct access to the beach. Double rooms are priced from £62 ($107); singles from £44 ($75).

"San Antonio" Hotel (****), Playa de los Pocillos, Tel: 82 50 50. 336 rooms with doubles priced from £73.

Aparthotel "Playa Grande" (**), Playa de los Pocillos, Tel: 82 52 27. 544 rooms/apartments priced around £37 ($63).

"El Dorado" Apartment House (three keys), Calle Graciosa, Tel: 82 53 63. 80 apartments priced from £24 ($50).

"Cabrera" Apartment House (two keys), Avenida las Playas 66. 20 apartments priced from £22 ($38).

"Lanzamar" Apartment House (two keys), Guardilama, Tel: 82 50 08. 112 apartments from £28 ($47).

"Las Vistas" Apartment House (two keys), Urbanización Playa Blanca, Tel: 82 50 08. 73 apartments from £26 ($44).

"Colina del Sol" Apartment House (one key), Puerto del Carmen, Tel: 82 52 75. 227 apartments priced from £33 ($57).

"San Francisco II" Apartment House (one key), Calle Teide, Tel: 82 61 00. 72 apartments priced from £22 ($38).

"Los Volcanes" Apartment House (three keys), Calle Alegranca, Tel: 82 50 33. 64 apartments priced from £22 ($38).

"Conjunto Residencial la Peita" Apartment House (two keys), Puerto del Carmen, Tel: 82 58 69. 215 apartments priced from £22 ($38).

"Costa Luz" Apartments (two keys), Playa de los Pocillos. 42 apartments priced from £22 ($38).

"Fariones Beach" Apartments (two keys), Avenida de las Playas. 28 apartments priced from £37 to £48 ($63 to $82).

"Los Hibiscos" Apartments (two keys), Calle Doramas, Tel: 82 59 08. 144 apartments priced from £33 ($57).

"Jable" Apartments (two keys), Calle Doramas, Tel: 82 50 04. 140 apartments priced from £22 ($38).

"Kon-Tiki" Apartments (two keys), Calle Guanapay, Tel: 82 59 50. 110 apartments priced from £40 ($69).

"Luz del Mar" Apartments (two keys), Avenida de las Playas, Tel: 82 58 69. 90 apartments priced from £22 ($38).

"Playa Mar" Apartments (two keys), Avenida Maritima 33, Tel: 82 57 02. 48 apartments priced from £26 ($44).

"San Francisco Park" Apartments (two keys), Calle Chalana, Tel: 82 61 60. 40 apartments priced from £22 ($38).

"Las Vegas" Apartments (two keys), Calle Chalana, Tel: 82 61 60. 18 apartments priced from £33 (57).

"Aries" Apartments (one key), Calle General Prim. 8 apartments priced from £26 ($44).

"Jardines San Antonio I, II, and III" (one key), Avenida de las Playas. The buildings here house 23 apartments in total priced around £20 ($35).

Car Rental

Autos Riverol, Urbanización Costa Luz near the San Antonio Hotel, Tel: 82 57 04; and Carretera de Tias, Tel: 82 52 29, 82 51 28 and 82 60 71.

Autos Cabrera Medina, Avenida las Playas, Tel: 82 58 76; Juan Carlos I No. 6, Tel: 82 62 38; Club del Carmen, Playa Pocillos, Tel: 82 55 53.

In addition, there is a car rental agency at the supermarket at Calle Timanfaya. Rental price is around £4.75 ($8.25) per day not including insurance.

"Lanzexpress", on the main street in Playa Blanca with good weekly rental prices.

"Bantayga Rent-a-Car", Avenida de las Playas, Playa Blanca.

Entertainment

"Bourbon Street Nite Spot", Calle Roque Nublo. Live music and dancing every evening from 7:30, no admission, drinks are priced from £1.10 ($1.90).

"LTU Pub", Avenida de las Playas, showing a German sports programme on Sundays with German beer on tap.

"Waikiki Beach Club", Hawaiian music and cocktails served as early as 11 am. Located on Avenida de las Playas.

"Porky's Disco Pub" and "Beach Club Discotheque" are both on Avenida de las Playas.

Medical Care

British Scandinavian Clinic, Avenida de las Playas, on call 24 hours.
"San Antonio" Emergency Clinic, Carretera Las Playas (Tias). Tel: 82 57 98.
Clinic Dr. Martin, Avenida de Las Playas, Tel: 82 59 11.

Pharmacies

Farmacia Centro, Calle Bajamar, Tel: 82 57 31.
Farmacia Rijo, Centro Commercial Costa Luz (San Antonio), Tel: 82 53 98.

Restaurants

The "Mundia Lanza" Restaurant is located on the right-hand side of the road
from Puerto del Carmen heading north to Macher. It is widely known for its
reasonably priced grilled specialities: a platter with port cutlets, bratwurst and
a hamburger costs around £5.50 ($9.50). There is a lunch buffet on Sundays
beginning at 1 pm priced around £4 ($7) per person.

Lanzarote: an absolute paradise for windsurfers, sailing enthusiasts and hikers

Pizzeria "Capriccio", corner of Calle Roque Nublo and Calle Gomera. Tip: the spaghetti is excellent.

"El Barco" and "Dionysios" Restaurants, both in the Centro Commercial Roque Nublo.

"Grill Suizo", Calle Roque Nublo.

Pizzeria "Roma", across from the taxi stand in the district of Playa Blanca; nice atmosphere catering to a British clientele.

Pizzeria "Balali", prices are reasonable but one must count on a long wait.

Shopping

"El Patio Center", somewhat north of Puerto del Carmen. Includes the "La Finca" Restaurant, a gallery, a ceramics shop, a flower shop and language school. The centre is open from 10 am to 1 pm and 5 to 8 pm; closed Sundays.

"Centro Commercial Roque Nublo", Calle Roque Nublo, with shops, restaurants and discotheques.

Calle Timanfaya and Calle Arrecife are the bazaar streets in the Playa Blanca district.

Sports and Recreation

"Castellana" Sports Center, Calle Guanapay, charges £3.30 ($5.75) for squash court fees per half hour per person. This centre also has sauna facilities.

Barakuda Club Diving Center, shortly before Matagorda, Tel: 82 57 65.

Windsurfing: "Los Dolphines" surfing school is located on Playa de Matagorda northwest of Puerto del Carmen. The wind is somewhat stronger here; however, even novices will be able to try their luck on a surfboard here. Surfboard rental per week costs £91 ($157); per day £28 ($47); and £5.50 ($9.50) per hour. A complete surfing course costs £73 ($125); a twelve-hour introduction, £55 ($94) and the one-hour introductory offer costs £14 ($24).

Pedal boats can also be rented at the "Los Dolphines" surfing school for £5.50 ($9.50) per hour. The same price is applicable to a fifteen-minute jet-ski rental.

Important Addresses

Currency Exchange: Banco de Bilbao, Caleton del Barranquillo, Tel: 82 59 26 and 82 59 27.

Banco Central, Calle Juan Carlos I 46, Tel: 82 51 73.

Banco Exterior de España, Puerto del Carmen s/n, Tel: 82 53 30 & 82 53 31.

Banco de las Islas Canarias, Calle Reina Sofia 1, Tel: 82 57 73.

Banco de Santander, Avenida Maritima las Playas 46, Tel: 82 51 27.
Post Office: Calle Bajamar 17, and Calle Roque Nublo 13.
Beach Chairs: can be rented at the beach on Avenida de las Playas. One costs £2.20 ($3.75) and two cost £3.30 ($5.75) per day.
Iberia Airlines: Avenida de las Playas.
Bus Stop: Calle Juan Carlos I.
Police: Guardia Civil, Juan Carlos I, Tel: 82 52 36.

Punta de Mujeres

Beyond Arrieta along the eastern coast of Lanzarote, a road leads north along the coastline toward Jameos del Agua and Orzola, Lanzarote northernmost city. Shortly beyond Arrieta, a road leads off to the right to the fishing village of Punta de Mujeres. This village is made up of a long stretch of coastal road with houses to either side.
The fishermen are increasingly concentrating on tourism today. There is no beach, but there are several shallow natural pools. In addition Punta de Mujeres' coastline offers good fishing.

Punta de Mujeres / **Practical Information**

Restaurants: The road into town leads past the "Tipico Canario" and "Palenke" on the right-hand side of the road. Both restaurants serve fish dishes, reasonably priced around £3.75 ($6.25).
Telephone: There is a telephone in the "Palenke" Restaurant.

Punta Pechiguera

Departing from Playa Blanca, a road leads off toward Punta Pechiguera after around 1 kilometre (½ mile). After driving 2 kilometres (1¼ miles), one will pass by ruins on the beach and the Montaña Roja on the opposite side of the road.
This reddish volcanic cone rises gradually to an elevation of 194 metres (635 feet). Bungalows and rows of houses were built along this route which leads only to the Faro Pechiguera lighthouse. This lighthouse marks the south-western extreme of Lanzarote. A visit to this point is recommended either on foot or by bicycle. The lighthouse is 5 kilometres (3 miles) from the town of Playa Blanca.

Radio

BBC World Service and Voice of America can be received on short-wave radios during the night and early morning.

Religion

Spain is a predominantly Catholic country. The majority of the residents of the Canary Islands are also Catholic.

Restaurants

Food and drink are served in the "bars" and the "restaurantes". In this guide, they are referred to as "bar-restaurantes".

In the bar "tapas" are usually served. These are small snacks for between meals, costing up to about £2 ($3.50). The bars also serve different types of coffee: black, coffee with milk, espresso or coffee with a shot of liqueur or Cognac. Most bars open at 9 am at the latest because this is when the working class eats breakfast. Women can only rarely be seen in the bars, although they are not officially unwelcome. Lunch or dinner in the restaurants cost from £5 ($9) to £7 ($12) including an appetiser, a main course, dessert and a beverage. Water is served with every meal upon request: normal drinking water is not always added to the bill; mineral water, on the other hand, always is charged extra. It is served in large bottles.

Bread is a part of every meal. Sometimes an extra charge for bread is added to the bill. If this happens, one should definitely complain if the price is unreasonable. →*also individual entries*

Roque del Este →*Isletas*
Roque del Oueste →*Isletas*
Salinas de Janubio →*Janubio*

San Bartolomé

The folk dancing group from the village of San Bartolomé (population: 3,000) is famous all across the island. The women wear large straw hats; unmarried girls, cloth bonnets. San Bartolomé is accessible from Puerto del Carmen via Tias after around 11 kilometres (7 miles) and from Arrecife via a good road

A shady spot in front of the beautiful church of San Bartolome

after around 5 kilometres (3 miles). The "Barracca II" Restaurant, the Guardia Civil and a pharmacy are all located on Avenida las Palmeras. Also on this street across from the supermarket is the "Caja Insular" where one can exchange money. A service station can be found in the centre of town as can a post box on Plaza León y Castillo where the church is located. The city hall and "Ganigo" bazaar where one can purchase souvenirs and groceries are also on this plaza. From San Bartolomé, it is only a few yards to the →*Monumento al Campesino*. One leaves town heading northeast toward Mozaga to find the monument, a creation of →*César Manrique,* on the left after passing a service station.

Important Addresses
Tourist Information/City Hall: Cervantes 4, Tel: 81 29 18.
Currency Exchange: Caja Insular de Ahorros, Tumbaiba s/n., Tel: 81 19 44.
Police: Joes M. Gil 8, Tel: 81 17 11; Cervantes 4, Tel: 81 29 18

Ship Travel → *Travelling to Lanzarote, Travel on Lanzarote*

Shopping

No one can conclusively say when stores are open. One must try one's luck – the best times are Monday to Friday from 9 am to 1 pm and from 4 to 7 or 8 pm; Saturdays from 9 am to 1 pm. During the Siesta between 1 and 4 pm, nothing much takes place – even some of the churches close during this time. "Calados", the filigree needlework is not only available on Tenerife. This is, along with baskets and leather goods, a typical souvenir from the islands. "Toledo" crafts – inlaid metal – are also very lovely, but not always authentic. That which feels smooth rather than rough is most likely plastic.

"Made in Cuba" on rum bottles and cigarillos does not always mean that this is true. The local products are sometimes "upgraded" in this way; however, their quality is still quite respectable.

On the beaches, peddlers sell "authentic gold Swiss watches". However, even within the free-trade zone of the Canary Islands, gold and jewels are not free. Reputable shops in the larger cities may be somewhat more expensive, but purchasing jewellery here will prevent disappointments later. "Authentic Guan-che weapons" are usually neither authentic nor are they good imitations. These are usually copies of fake "originals".

Alcohol, perfume, and tobacco products are inexpensive on the islands because they are duty-free. One is well advised to buy these articles before the return flight because the duty-free shops in the airports – if there are any at all – are usually more expensive than the shops in the cities. Duty-free items purchased aboard the airplane will definitely be more expensive than on the Canaries.

There are numerous shops for those who choose to cook for themselves. Supermarkets will have everything that is available in central Europe, even though these items will be more expensive.

Bargains can be found in the unpretentious shops in the small towns outside of the tourist centres. There, one can buy the basic foods, figs, wine etc. for up to 50% less than in the cities.

Sights

Lanzarote is worth seeing merely by virtue of the fact that it is volcanic in origin. Those travelling on this island to experience its natural beauty will never cease to be amazed. Geological highlights include the Timanfaya National Park with its →*Montañas del Fuego,* the mountains of fire. The volcanic grottoes to the northeast →*Jameos del Agua* and →*Cueva de los Verdes* count as natural wonders. →*El Golfo* is also of volcanic origin as is the rugged coastline of →*Los Hervideros.*

Also holding a fascination all their own are the craters of →*La Geria,* the main area for wine production. This region provides an impression of just how hard the Lanzarotan farmers must work to coax such quality grapes from this arid soil. The →*Cochenille,* the cochineal lice used in the production of a red pigment used for lipstick also count among the fascinating agricultural products of Lanzarote. These lice live on cactus plants found in the largest numbers in the →*Mala* and →*Guatiza* regions. Working the land is hard. Thus, it is not surprising that →*César Manrique* dedicated a monument to Lanzarote's farming population: the →*Monumento al Campesino.* The name of this artist and architect is inseparably linked to the island of Lanzarote. He fought for and won in an initiative to prohibit advertising on the entire island. César Manrique lived in the house belonging to the "César Manrique Foundation" which he founded in 1982. Now this building is open to the public. The foundation presents sketches, paintings, drawings, sculptures and objects from this artist's life's work. Admission costs around £5 ($8.45)

Soo

Soo is a village south of Costa Blanca in Lanzarote's northern regions – a typical drive-through town. One can, however, reach the La Isleta peninsula from Soo via a byway or continue on to La Caleta de Famara. Soo lives from agriculture. The neighbouring volcanic cones of the Montaña Mosta, Pico Colorado and Soo (which lent the town its name; elevation 293 metres/958 feet) are of geological interest. The "La Entrada" Café can be found in the centre of town serving not only coffee, but snacks and light meals as well.

Speed Limits

On motorways 120 kmph, on thoroughfares 100 kmph and on two-lane country roads 90 kmph are permitted. Within towns and cities, 50 kmph is permitted as long as there is no sign stating otherwise. Cars towing trailers may not exceed 70 kmph, on motorways 80 kmph and on thoroughfares 110 kmph.
Due to the poor conditions of many roads, one will not be able to drive much faster than an average speed of 35 kmph: the smaller roadways are usually unpaved and are not secured at the curves.

Sports and Recreation

The Canary Islands are a virtual paradise for sailing, surfing and hiking. Fishing is also possible, and along the harbours, deep-sea fishing tours are offered – shark fishing, for instance.
Tennis has become quite popular on the island. Tourist centres are equipped with tennis courts. Individual hotels often allow only club members to use their tennis facilities. However, one does have the option of becoming a club member for a limited amount of time, or be invited as a guest by a club member. Lanzarote in particular is very popular with wind surfers. The wind conditions on this island attract experts from around the world to challenge the sometimes rough surf. Novices will have a chance to learn this type of sport in a more tame context in →*Puerto del Carmen* for example, where one can not only rent surfboards but also take surfing lessons.

Tahiche

Tahiche lies between Arrecife and Teguise. If coming from San Bartolomé to Tahiche then one will pass by a beautiful crater across from the archaeological excavations on the right-hand side of the road.

The archaeological excavations are called Castillo de Zanzomas after the most important of the Canarian kings, the descendants of which did not exactly make life easy for the Spaniards (→*History*). The underground complex has been partially unearthed. Unfortunately, the excavated stone houses and plazas are usually driven by unnoticed because the crater on the other side of the road is more eye-catching. On second glance, the fascination of this volcano makes way for disenchantment. One drives through a gateway into the interior of the volcano – the rubbish heap of Lanzarote. Definitely a vivid answer to the question: where indeed does all of the rubbish go which is discarded by all of the tourists visiting Lanzarote? This crater is the solution

Whether on foot or taking a bus — Lanzarote's sights and landscapes make the trip worthwhile

to Lanzarote's waste disposal problems, even though it does involve unpleasant odours when the wind changes.

This did not prevent the famous artist → *César Manrique* from building a house in Tahiche, which – as rumour has it – could be used as a museum after the death of the master artist and architect.

Tao

Tao, located at the base of the 550 metre (1,800 foot) volcanic cone also called Tao, can be reached by taking the route between Mozaga and Tiagua. Shortly after driving into town from the south is the bus stop. Only a little farther to the right is a sign for the "Don Miguel de Tao" restaurant. This restaurant is widely known for its grill specialities. The restaurant is closed Mondays.

Tajarte→ *Tinajo*

Teguise

Teguise is the old capital city of Lanzarote. It was named after the daughter of a Guanche king who married Maciot de Bethancourt, the nephew of the conqueror Jean de Bethancourt. Maciot was the regent of the island for many years even though he only administrated Lanzarote for his uncle *(→History)*. Teguise has the character of a museum and simply exudes history, a history which began for this city during the 15th century. Up to 1852, Teguise was the island's capital and the bishop's seat.

The residents felt safe from pirate attacks here in the island's interior. It only happened once in 1586 that Algerians penetrated to Teguise and set fire to the city. Then the English came to Teguise. While the Thirty Years' War broke out in Europe, North Africans caused chaos in Teguise, burned the city to the ground and killed men, women and children. The Callejon de Sangre, the "alleyway of blood", is a reminder of this tragic chapter in the history of this beautiful city.

Teguise is home to a population of around 6,000. Today, Teguise attracts hundreds of visitors every day. Old buildings from the Spanish era remain preserved although their uses today are much different from their original functions. This city could very plausibly be somewhere in Mexico. A massive church called "San Miguel" built in 1680 stands at the centre of this city. Within the church is a madonna statue. When it was said to have been stolen many years ago, legend has it that a dog drove the thief out of the city. In front of the church on the expansive plaza, stone lions guard the cathedral. Their eyes are fixed on the Palacio Spinola. Earlier, the Captain General resided in this palace; today, it houses a cultural centre with a museum. Admission is around 30p (50¢). Also taking place here on a regular basis are art exhibits with works by Canarian artists as well as festivals, lectures and theatre performances.

Between the San Miguel Church and the cultural centre, the "Caja Canarias" Bank is now housed in an old storehouse. Right near the plaza, one can also find various shops, among them a handicrafts shop.

The Sunday market taking place between 8 am and 4 pm is worth the trip to Teguise, offering a cross-section of Canarian folklore in addition to agricultural produce, ceramics, wickerwork and baskets and stands with snacks and tapas.

Teguise makes a prosperous impression and this can be mainly attributed to the present mayor Dimas Martin and his "onion affair". He introduced the Sunday market to Teguise and founded a cooperative which dominated the entire onion market on Lanzarote and sold up to 2,000 tons of onions annually. In addition, he played a decisive role in bringing about the construction of the Costa Teguise holiday complex.

Worth seeing in this region: Castillo Santa Barbara (also called Castillo de Guanapay). Admission is 200 pesetas. "Timples" musical instruments similar to a small guitar are produced in the workshops of Teguise.

Teguise / **Practical Information**

Pharmacy: Licenciada Carmen Repollez, Calle Juan Melian, Tel: 84 52 84.

Restaurants: Bar-Restaurante "Galería", Calle Victor Feo, Tel: 84 50 36; located somewhat off the beaten track but accessible from the plaza. The prices are acceptable, the portions generous and the chefs stick to traditional Canarian recipes. On the walls are pictures by foreign artists who have settled on the island – thus the name of this restaurant.

The Bar-Restaurante "Acative" across from the church is one of the oldest in Teguise. One can also purchase souvenirs in the same building as well as hearing lectures. On Sundays, the atmosphere is bustling after the church services. This building also serves as the setting for dance evenings on occasion.

A small café can be found at the old "San Francisco de Miraflores" Franciscan monastery which dates back to the 16th century as well as at the Santo Domingo" monastery which the Dominicans had built during the 18th century. These two buildings can be seen when driving from the centre of town toward Castillo de Guanapay and Mirador del Rio.

Important Addresses
Currency Exchange: Caja Insular de Ahorros, Calle Doctor Alfonso Espinola s/n., Tel: 84 52 02.
Tourist Information/City Hall: Plaza General Franco 3, Tel: 84 50 01 and 84 50 72.
Police: Plaza General Franco 3, Tel: 84 50 01.

Telephone

When placing an international call: dial 07, then wait for a high-pitched tone, and continue by dialling the country code and the number.

Country Codes:

Australia — 07.61.	New Zealand — 07.64.
Canada — 07.1.	United Kingdom – 07.44;
Ireland — 07.353.	United States — 07.1.

It can take a while for the connection to be established. International calls can be placed from public telephones marked "internacionales". One must, however, carry a large amount of change. Newer public telephones also accept telephone cards. A two-minute call to Europe costs around £1.50 ($2.65) (→Postal System).

Theatre →*Entertainment*

Theft

Although the Canary Islands are among the most frequently visited holiday destinations for middle and northern Europeans, this has hardly led to an increase in crime. Even in the larger centres on Tenerife and Gran Canaria, there is little to criticise.

One qualification: Las Palmas de Gran Canaria. It is a big city with marked social contrasts. Owing to the fact that Las Palmas is one of the largest harbours in Europe, it consistently attracts illegal immigrants. They can blend in well among all of the tourists here. The principles of a big city are in effect in Las Palmas. Leaving a rental car unlocked is ill-advised. Even leaving luggage in a locked car is not a good idea.

Hotels will usually offer the use of a safe in which valuables can be deposited. Expensive articles should by all means be stored in a safe, even if this service does cost a few extra pesetas per day. The peace of mind is well worth the extra money. Travel insurance covering theft is also recommended, in case something is stolen despite the precautions (→*Insurance*, →*Conduct, Embassies and Consulates, Police*)

Tiagua

To reach Tiagua, drive southwest toward Uga and turn right near Mozaga. After 5 kilometres (3 miles) one will reach the village of Tiagua beyond Tao. Just after driving into town, one will see the "Tiagua" restaurant on the left-hand side and shortly after that, a public telephone as well as a post box at a grocery store. The chapel and the old windmill of Tiagua can be seen along the street which leads off to the right from the main road to Soo.

Only cultivated plants lend some colour to the bleak grey of Lanzarote's volcanic landscapes

Tias

Tias lies 12 kilometres (7½ miles) west of Arrecife along the GC 720 roadway. The residents of Tiagua live predominantly from agriculture; the town itself is otherwise less significant. On the way from Puerto del Carmen to San Bartolomé, one will pass through Tias. The bus stop for buses heading to Arrecife and Puerto del Carmen is at the church.

Important Addresses

Tourist Information/City Hall: Carretera General 74, Tel: 82 50 22.
Currency Exchange: Caja Insular de Ahorros, León y Castillo 51, Tel: 82 50 78.
Car Rental: Autos Riverol, Tel: 82 51 28 and 82 51 29.
Police: Carretera General 74, Tel: 82 50 22.

Time of Day

The clocks seem to run differently on the Canary Islands. For instance, dinner is served quite late, although the population has meanwhile adapted to the tourists – dinner is now also served somewhat earlier. From 1 to 4 pm is the siesta time. It can happen that in the early afternoon shops are closed – this is even true for the churches

The time of day on the Canary Islands is the same as in Great Britain (Greenwich Mean Time) and one hour later than in Central Europe. It is 5 (New York) to 8 hours (Los Angeles) later than in the continental United States.

Tinajo

Tinajo lies in the island's northeastern regions between the Montaña del Fuego and the La Isleta Peninsula. Tinajo is accessible from Arrecife via Mozaga, Tao and Tiagua on the road GC 740. When entering town from this direction, one will see the "Tinajo" Restaurant on the left-hand side, especially recommended for grilled dishes.

There is a grocery store across from the restaurant and the city hall, the taxi stand and the "La Plaza" Bar on the plaza before the church. On the road to Montaña del Fuego is one of Lanzarote's few cinemas predominantly showing films in the Spanish language. There is a post office on the right-hand side of the road. After a few hundred yards, almost in Mancha Blanca, one will see the Montaña del Tinajo crater to the right, the rim of which is 189 metres (618 feet) high.

Adjacent to Tinajo are the towns of Tajarte, Casas de Guignon and Mancha Blanca. All of these towns are predominantly dependent on agriculture. La Mancha Blanca is the last settlement, 3 kilometres (2 miles) from the centre of Tinajo. At this point, one road leads off to the left towards La Vagueta and Tiagua. The Ermita de los Dolores lies on this road. The statue of Mary in the chapel is venerated across the entire island. Also due to the occasional crowds of visitors around the building, ample parking was provided for. The "El Volcan" Bar is an inviting stop after visiting the church.

Important Addresses

Tourist Information/City Hall: Plaza San Roque 1, Tel: 84 00 21.
Police: Plaza San Roque 1, Tel: 84 00 21.
Taxis: Plaza San Roque, Tel: 84 00 49.

Tipping

As a general rule, hotels add 15% to the total amount for service. Waiters, porters, room service and maid service do expect a tip of around 15%, which should serve as orientation in restaurants. However, since a tip is an acknowledgement of good service, keep in mind that poor service should not be rewarded no matter where one might be.

Also tipped are: taxi drivers, camel guides, ushers in cinemas and theatres and also the curators and supervisors at various points of interest.

Toilets

There are very few public toilets on the Canary Islands. Those in a pinch should not hesitate to go into one of the bars. Those who find this brash can clear their conscience by ordering an espresso, which usually costs no more than around 17p (30¢).

Some bar owners lock the facilities when the proprietor realises that his customers make a "relieved" impression, but the cash register remains empty. Understandable enough.

There are two types of toilets on the Canary Islands: the type to sit on and the type to squat above. Both have their advantages and drawbacks, although the squat toilets can take some getting used to.

Beside the toilet is usually a bin, not only used for sanitary napkins and tampons. Toilet paper should not be flushed down the toilet but placed in this bin. This prevents the pipes from stopping up. Keep in mind that water is scarce on the islands; saving water is a virtue among tourists. In the showers, one will note that water pressure is usually insufficient.

Tourist Information

Information is available from the Spanish Tourist Information Offices:

In Great Britain
57-58 Saint James Street
London,
SW1 1DL
Tel: (01) 499 09 01

In the United States
 - 665 5th Avenue
New York, NY 10022
Tel: (212) 759-8822
Fax: (212) 980-1053
 - Water Tower Place, #915
845 N. Michigan Avenue
Chicago, IL 60611
Tel: (312) 642-1992

 - 1221 Brickel Avenue
Miami, FL 33131
Tel: (305) 358-1992
Fax: (305) 536-1236
8383 Wilshire Blvd., Suite 960
 - Beverly Hills, CA 90211
Tel: (213) 658-7188
Fax: (213) 658-1061

In Canada
102 Bloor Street W, 14th Floor
Toronto, Ontario M5S 1M8
Tel: (416) 961-3131
Fax: (416) 961-1992

Traffic Regulations

One is only allowed to parallel park in the direction of traffic. When parking in an one way street, on even numbered days, one must park on the side of the street with the even numbered houses, otherwise on the other side.
Many of the traffic regulations are similar to those in other countries, but the regulation giving the vehicle coming from the right the right of way can be applied more often – especially on traffic circles. At night, vehicles may only drive with low-beams, at dusk with parking lights other than on the throughways and motorways.
One is not only allowed to honk the horn when driving into a curve, one should do this for one's own safety as well. Horn honking is prohibited in cities between 11 pm and 6 am.
There is still no breakdown service available and towing with private vehicles is prohibited. Vehicles which have broken down must be towed by towing

companies. It is not allowed to overtake cars on streets or 100 metres (110 yards) before streets with a visibility of less than 200 metres (220 yards). A driver who sticks his left hand out of the window is signalling that he or she is stopping for pedestrians.

Travel Documents

For a stay of up to 90 days, citizens of EC member states and most other werstern nations need only valid identity card to enter Lanzarote; all other visitors must have a valid passport. When travelling by car, one should always carry a passport; should a police officer request identification, it is better to have it along than saying it is in the hotel. A passport is also required in the following situations: cashing traveller's cheques (or Eurocheques), checking into hotels or other accommodation, registering with the police (when staying longer than 90 days) and when renting a car. A national driving licence and an international insurance card is necessary when bringing one's own car to the Canary Islands. Those who wish to bring pets along must have health certification for the animal or at least proof of rabies vaccination translated into Spanish. The vaccination must have taken place at least 30 days and at most one year prior to entering the Canary Islands. This certification must be notarised by a Spanish consulate before departure *(→Embassies and Consulates)*. Documents for pets which have not been notarised are only accepted if issued by a governmental or officially recognised veterinarian.

Travel on Lanzarote

The most comfortable way of getting around on the Canary Islands is by car *(→Car Rental)* since the *→buses* do not always operate regularly and do not always go to every town that one might want to visit. Those who bring their own car or motorcycle will need an international insurance card and will also have to affix a nationality sticker to the vehicle.

In the larger towns there is always at least one service station. The fuel supply is sufficient so there is no need to bring along a canister of fuel, which is also subject to duty. The service stations are closed on Sundays and holidays. Those who would like to avoid unpleasant surprises should always fill the fuel tank before the weekend.

Fuel prices per litre: normal 92 octane = 35p (65¢); super 97 octane = 37p (68¢); diesel (gasoleo "A") = 23p (44¢). Almost all stations also provide lead-free fuel at 43p (81¢). Hitchhiking is always a matter of luck, even on Tenerife. Many tourists rent a car so that they can travel independently. A hitchhiker, who wants to travel around the island for free, might be viewed as being quite brash.

There is no train on any of the Canary Islands, but there are quite a few taxi drivers. A taxi will charge a flat rate of £2 ($3.75); for a longer trip, 43p (81¢) per kilometre. Every taxi driver has a list of fixed prices for longer distances which must not be exceeded which must be shown upon request. For self-determined routes, it is advisable to negotiate the price in advance.

The following taxi prices are intended to serve as an orientation and are valid for trips from Puerto del Carmen, one of the largest tourist centres on Lanzarote. Listed below are taxi routes and prices for Lanzarote's main towns which can be found listed alphabetically in this guide.

Airport	11 km (7 miles)	£4.75 ($8.25)
Arrecife	15 km (9 miles)	£6.55 ($11.25)
Costa Teguise	24 km (15 miles)	£10.25 ($17.50)
Nazaret	25 km (15 miles)	£10.55 ($18.25)
Teguise	21 km (13 miles)	£9.10 ($15.65)
Jameos del Agua	45 km (28 miles)	£18.20 ($31.25)
Mirador del Rio	50 km (31 miles)	£20 ($34.40)
Macher	5 km (3 miles)	£3 ($5)
Tias	5 km (3 miles)	£3 ($5)
Montañas del Fuego	25 km (15 miles)	£10.55 ($18.25)
El Golfo	25 km (15 miles)	£10.55 ($18.25)
Playa Blanca	30 km (19 miles)	£12.40 ($21.25)

There are two options to travel to the neighbouring islands: Iberia Airline flights or Trasmediterranea ships departing from Arrecife's harbour and taking passengers to the main cities on the neighbouring islands.

Iberia flights from Lanzarote depart daily for Gran Canaria, Fuerteventura and Tenerife. From there, connecting flights to La Palma and El Hierro are available. The single flight between two neighbouring islands costs around £22 ($37.50).

Travelling by ship is somewhat less expensive. Depending on the season, there are ferries departing on for Las Palmas de Gran Canaria three or four times weekly and just as many to Santa Cruz de Tenerife. From Tenerife, one can then easily take the Ferry Gomera to the island of La Gomera as well as ferries to El Hierro and La Palma departing three times per week. The single trip between two neighbouring islands costs around £18.20 ($31.25).

Fuerteventura is accessible by taking the "Alisur" ferry (Tel: 81 42 72 and 81 49 01) from Playa Blanca. This is worthwhile even if only spending one day. The "Alisur S.A." ferry company was founded in 1981. At that time it operated a catamaran between the main cities on the Canary Islands: first from Arrecife to Puerto del Rosario on Fuerteventura and later to La Graciosa as well. Then the owners had the idea of establishing a ferry line between Corralejo on Fuerteventura and Playa Blanca on Lanzarote, creating a connection which immediately met with the approval of passengers. It is hardly possible to find a quicker and more convenient way of taking a trip to Fuerteventura. In 1986, 96,000 passengers took advantage of the ferry connections offered by the "Alisur" company.

"Alisur" ships depart from Playa Blanca daily for the harbour city of Corralejo on Fuerteventura passing the island of Lobos along the way.

Departure times from Playa Blanca to Corralejo: 7:20 and 9:40 am; 5:00 pm.
Departure times from Corralejo to Playa Blanca: 8:30 and 10:50 am; 6:20 pm.
In addition the competing "Ferry Betancuria" company also offers service along this route.
Departure times from Playa Blanca to Corralejo: 9:00 and 11:00 am; 3:30 and 6:00 pm.
Departure times from Corralejo to Playa Blanca: 8:00 and 10:00 am; 2:30 and 5:00 pm.
The trip costs around £8.25 ($14) each way with a 50% discount for children up to 12 years of age. There is no charge for children under two. A return ticket costs twice the single fare.

The "Alisur" company also transports vehicles for the prices listed below:

Vehicle Length	Single Trip	Return Trip
under 4 m (under 13'1")	£13.50 ($23.15)	£21.85 ($37.50)
4.1 to 4.5 m (13'5" to 14'8")	£16.40 ($28.15)	£24.40 ($41.90)
over 4.51 m (over 14'9")	£19.00 ($32.50)	£29.90 ($51.25)
motorcycles	£8.00 ($13.75)	£13.50 ($23.15)

Additional addresses of shipping lines:
"Alisur": Arrecife, León y Castillo 16 and Centro C El Mercadillo 19. Aucona Trasmediterranea: Arrecife, Muelle de los Marmoles s/n., Tel: 81 11 74.
Fred Olsen Lines: Arrecife, Triana 23, Tel: 81 11 79.
The main Iberia Airline offices: Arrecife, Avenida Mancomunidad s/n., Tel: 81 03 50 and Av. del Generalismo Franco 10, Tel: 81 03 50.

Travelling to Lanzarote

Lanzarote has become such a popular holiday destination on the Canary Islands and in Spain that the airport on Lanzarote has problems handling all of the passengers.
From London, a flight to Lanzarote Airport costs around £220 ($380) depending on the season and based on a stay of up to one month. If staying longer, the flight can increase by about £65 ($115). Charter flights usually require that the date of the return flight is set in advance. These flights are usually booked as part of a package tour, meaning that accommodation is also included. One is less committed with "camping flights", which include hotel vouchers: one can then arrange accommodation after arriving on Lanzarote.
The least expensive way to get to the island is by booking a "last minute flight" which, of course, does not literally imply that the flight takes place at the last minute but does require some flexibility. As a rule, these kind of offers are package tours. Prices for the flight vary between £100 ($187) and £134 ($250). The trip to Lanzarote by ship from Cadiz in southern Spain takes about two and a half days. The route is via Las Palmas de Gran Canaria and Santa Cruz de Tenerife arriving in Arrecife. This does offer one advantage in that an automobile can also be transported. This costs between £50 ($94) and £160 ($300) depending on the length of the vehicle with an additional charge of between £114 ($213) and £217 ($408) per person (children pay half of the adult fare). Taking a motorcycle costs from £20 to £30 ($38 to $56) each way. The current schedule for departures and prices can be obtained from travel agencies, who will also be able to arrange bookings. With the exception of La Gomera, all of the Canary Islands have airports. In summer 1991, the cornerstone was laid for an airport on La Gomera, but its completion is planned for 1997. So in a few years Lanzarote will be accessible from all of the Canary Islands by air (→ *Travel on Lanzarote*). The harbour of Arrecife can be reached by ferry from Rosario (Fuerteventura), Las Palmas de Gran Canaria and Santa Cruz de Tenerife. The ship line offering this service is the Compañia Trasmediterranea, with offices located at each of the harbours served.

There are connections from Corralejo on Fuerteventura to Playa Blanca on Lanzarote offered by the "Alisur" and "BETANCURIA" companies. For further information → _Travel on Lanzarote_.

Uga

Uga is the traffic hub in the southern regions of Lanzarote. The main road leads off to the east to the airport and Arrecife; to the west, the road goes via Yaiza to Playa Blanca; and to the northwest, the road northwest to Teguise. In tourist brochures, it is said that one will feel as if in Africa when visiting Uga. However, it is not apparent why this should be the case unless it is because of the 100 dromedaries used for the ride into the Mountains of Fire and tended to by Western African and Canarian keepers.

Oranges thrive behind the high walls. In the "Timanfaya" Restaurant which can be especially recommended for breakfast, there is also a souvenir shop. The owner here also owns the dromedaries. The "Isidro Labrador" celebrates

Many of the Canary Island's residents live predominantly from agriculture as can be seen here from the onion fields

its consecration on May 15. Both across from and behind the church, there is a public telephone as well as a taxi stand.

Those who take a trip to Uga should ask directions to Bodega "Betancourt". This wine cellar offers a selection of wines pressed from grapes grown on Lanzarote's volcanic soil.

Vaccinations

No vaccinations are required for those travelling to the Canary Islands. It is, however, a good idea to check into the date of the last tetanus vaccination since it is very easy to injure oneself on the sharp volcanic rocks in the Malpaises or even on the beach.

Vegetation

Although the discovery of the Canary Islands dates back more than 400 years and the fact that exploitation of the natural resources – especially the vegetation – was carried out to a considerable degree, the general vegetation is very rich in terms of endemic and imported plants. Botanists refer to the Canarian vegetation as a "macronic" region, also including the vegetation on the Azores and Cape Verde Islands. Here, plants from the African semi-deserts thrive as do the evergreen laurel forests on La Gomera and Gran Canaria. Even alpine plants thrive here such as the *Viola cheiranthifolia,* a pretty violet which grows only at the loftier elevations in the mountains of the Canary Islands. It grows in the pumice soils on the Pico del Teide on Tenerife. Banana plantations frequently appear in the form of monocultures, especially on the central and western islands. Eucalyptus grows on cleared slopes, xerophyten on caves at a height of about 300 metres (981 feet), lichen of the species *Lotus lancerottensis* on rocks near coast.

The Canary dragon tree *Dracaena Draco* is highly typical of these islands and some specimens are said to be more than 1,000 years old. However, this is a question of public relations in the first place, and secondly, it is very difficult to estimate the age of the trees. Dragon trees belong to the family of the agaves and lilies, and like palms they do not have growth rings. Therefore, their age can only be credibly estimated by their branches.

The wild dragon tree can be found on Tenerife, El Hierro, La Palma and Gran Canaria. It also exists in the fossilised form of the *Dracaena narbonnensis* in quarries in southern France.

The *Canary palm* is related to the north African date palm and a popular natural resource used in the production of mats and baskets. It thrives in humid regions. The island La Palma and several towns and canyons where named after this tree. On La Gomera, even honey and wine are made from the sap of palm trees. Palm groves can be found here and on La Palma.

The *date palm* was probably imported as well as the *grapevine* originally coming from Crete and Madeira.

In the 19th century, wine production was afflicted by the then unknown disease mildew, ending the boom on the island. Today, Canarian wines are a rarity.

The *Canary pine* grows in impressive forests on Tenerife, El Hierro, La Palma and Gran Canaria. It can reach a height of 40 to 60 metres (130 to 196 feet) and the diameter of the trunk is around 2.5 metres (8 feet). The needles reach a length of around 30 centimetres (1 foot) and are able to extract moisture from the clouds, doubling the water supplied to the roots. The wood is usually soft, and therefore, not very popular. There are, however, also dark pines with wood containing large amounts of resin and are resistant to insects. These share the characteristics of woods such as teak.

"Cardon" is the term used to describe *spurge plants*, which have the appearance of a candelabra. Some passers-by assume these to be cactus plants. These plants contain a large quantity of poisonous juice in their roots, fruit and branches, which is at the very least an eye irritant. The juice is said to have been used in the embalming of the Canarian mummies. A spurge plan grow up to 10 feet in diameter. It grows on all of the larger Canary Islands; however, not on the coast.

In 1820, the cochineal lice and the prickly pear were imported from Mexico. The cochineal produce a pigment used in the production of cosmetics. The farmers on the island feared that these lice would contaminate the feed for their livestock.

However, the cochineal were a true blessing for the islands: between 1831 and 1870, the export of this pigment producing louse increased from four kilograms to 300 metric tons. This was one fifth of the world production behind only Guatemala and Mexico. In 1877, it sank to 220 metric tons; in 1911, only small amounts were exported via Marseille to China. Since the end of the Second World War, twelve metric tons of cochineal have been used in the production of cosmetics. Today, only traces of this pigment can still be found in lipstick and other cosmetics. The Canary Islands produce enough of this pigment to meet the entire demand in Europe.

After the lice went out of fashion, the *banana* was the export hit. Banana liqueur is one of the island's specialities.

Cinerarias, chrysanthemums, succulent plants and *"viper heads"* (there are giant red-blossomed specimens on Tenerife) also grow on the islands – even sweet lemons grow here. *Fig, acacia* and *eucalyptus trees* were imported. The eucalyptus trees from Australia were mainly used to line the streets. *The Acacia trees* originate from South Africa or Australia, and the fig trees come from Australia, Africa, Asia or America.

Vegetation on Lanzarote

The plant life on Lanzarote seems desolate at first glance. Only cultivated plants like grapevines, orange trees, sometimes grains and of course the large opuntia cactuses bring some colour to the predominantly dark grey landscape. It is especially the eastern coast and the area around the airport which are anything but well suited to plant lovers. There are numerous halophytes, less attractive plants growing in the salty earth and in summer, one will notice the thorny bushes. The →*Timanfaya* region including the →*Montañas del Fuego* is, however, considered exemplary of how a suddenly barren, scorched landscape can bring forth new plant life – mosses and lichens at first. In a few thousand years, this area could support higher plants.

Lanzarote's vegetation has become more or less a diverse world of *grasses* when not considering the thorny bushes. Low shrubs have taken root especially to the north on the Famara coast near La Caleta. Botanists call these euphorbia salsola, suadea and launaea. This region is meanwhile of such scientific value that it is in discussion whether it should be declared a nature reserve due to its unusual flora.

Water

The water supply is one of the largest problems on the Canary Islands. Meanwhile, the tour organisations always point out that water shortages are possible. The major burden on the water supply is tourism. However, it is by no means so bad that the wells have run dry. The number of those using the water has doubled due to tourism.

In the early colonial period, water was still considered property of the privileged. Today, the allocation of the water is overseen by the "herades" which have been in existence on Gran Canaria since 1505. Surface water is used in agriculture and for the everyday demands of the populace.

However, especially on Tenerife in the Orotava Valley, in Cumbre de Pedro Gil, Candelaria and Güimar, there are "galerias". These tunnels are around 5 feet high and lead to the water table in the mountains. Most are ¼ to ½ mile long but they can measure up to 2½ miles (4 kilometres) in length. The total length of the galerias network on Tenerife is estimated at 630 miles (1,000 kilometres). Building these tunnels is a risk – some never produce water. Others, like the tunnels of Güimar on Tenerife, in contrast, contain so much water that they can supply the entire southern portion of the island via the "Canal de Sur".

In addition, there are deep wells ("pozos"). Motorised or wind-driven pumps bring water to the surface of Gran Canaria, Fuerteventura, Tenerife, La Gomera and La Palma from a depth of over 300 metres.

The largest reservoirs the "presas", can be found on Fuerteventura – the "Embalse de los Molinos;" and in the southwestern region of Gran Canaria – "Presa de la Chira", "Presa de la Niña" and "Presa de la Ayagaures".

Water on Lanzarote

The water supply is the number one problem on Fuerteventura and Lanzarote. While there are wells and sufficient precipitation on the islands of Tenerife, Gran Canaria, La Palma, El Hierro, and La Gomera the eastern islands called "Purpurarias" must budget strictly with their water supply. It is especially agriculture which must resort to farming methods unique throughout the world as is apparent through the example of La Geria.

For the tourist industry, this means that the package tour organisers already inform potential clientele that there can be water shortages during their stay. In fact, Lanzarote could barely supply its own resident population with water. However, the number of holiday visitors is a multiple of this. The distillation facilities near Arrecife meanwhile ensure the water supply of Lanzarote for the most part. Rain water is also collected but neither the one nor the other is suitable to drink. However in the supermarkets for only a few pesetas, water is available in two and five litre containers. "Firgas" is a brand one will encounter again and again. This water is brought over from Gran Canaria.

There are also several springs in the Famara region south of La Caleta which provide water for the households of Lanzarote. The tank vehicles which are in part painted blue usually pump the precious water into a water tank built on the roof of a house. From there, it flows directly or through filters to the kitchen or bathroom. Another thing one will see quite often, especially on Lanzarote are the extensive concrete areas with a depression at the centre. Below are the reservoirs for these cisterns.

Weights and Measures

On Lanzarote, as in all of Spain, the metric system is used including degrees Celsius. Most measures in this guide appear in both the metric and British system for the reader's convenience.

Wine

Lanzarote produces excellent malmsey wines which are also exported to other islands. The grapevines brought Lanzarote are a hearty variety which thrive in the barren soils on the Greek island of Crete.

Malvasia (malmsey) wines made the Portuguese island of Madeira, 500 kilometres (315 miles) to the north of Lanzarote, famous. According to legend, the English Duke George of Clarence was drown in a vat of this wine in 1478. Since he was condemned to death, he chose this means of bidding life adieu. When considering the price of this wine today, his last wish would probably not have been granted: one bottle of malvasia wine costs around £3.65 ($6.25) on Lanzarote.

The best malvasia wine was once that which was transported in a vat aboard a ship headed to East India, aging along the way; the so-called "East India Madeira". Today, the wine is heated to 60°C (140°F) after the first stage of fermentation in heated chambers called "estafados" in Portuguese. It is then sold as "vinho estufado".

The vines for these malvasia wines have been grown on the Canary Islands since the 15th century. Trade with this wine thrived in 1561 between the islands, England and India. During this time the grapevines were not yet grown on Lanzarote. It was first during the 18th century that this would change. The volcanoes erupted and covered 200 square kilometres (78 square miles) of the islands surface with volcanic ash. The fact that the malvasia vine thrives in this soil is a blessing for the island. Today, 3,300 hectares (8,250 acres) are used in cultivating grape vines; 1,931 hectares (4,828 acres) alone for the malvasia vines with Diego, Tinto and Muscatel vines covering the remaining areas. Grapes for white wines are grown on three-quarters of the area; the remainder is used for the production of red wines. Tending the vineyards is hard work. A depression 30 to 80 centimetres (12 to 20 inches) deep must be dug for each vine as can be seen in La Geria, the main area of cultivation. Small walls are then built around these craters to protect the plants from the wind. The grapes can only be harvested once a year in July and August. The grapes are then packed into crates of 20 kilograms (44 pounds) each, brought to the Bodegas (wine cellars) and carefully pressed. The must is then cooled, fermentation begins to later be filtered and filled into wooden vats. The sweetest wine results when grapes are first harvested at the end of August when they have reached their peak in sugar content. After fermenting ten days, the wine has an alcohol content of 12%. One of the most famous wine cellars on Lanzarote is "El Grifo". They produce a total of 300,000 bottles (700 ml) annually. However, even in the smaller gardens tended by farmers include grapevines. Their wines are then sold as house wines in shops and restaurants. The total production of wine on Lanzarote is around 1.2 million litres in bad years and around 2 million litres in good years with ample rainfall.

Yaiza

In the small rural city of Yaiza, dromedaries are kept for excursions to the fire mountains north of Yaiza. This is home to almost 2,000 residents living at an altitude of 190 metres (622 feet). There is also a sign for the "Guardia Civil" police station. Turning right at this sign, then one will reach the Montañas del Fuego, the mountains of fire, after about 7 kilometres (4½ miles). There is also a service station along this road.

Along the main street in Yaiza, there are various shops, one of which sells "Artesanía del Pais": embroidery, blouses and other handicrafts. In the "Bazar Boutique Artesanía Africana", artistic handicrafts from Africa are offered as souvenirs. These are indeed mass-produced items but they are still quite nice. And Lanzarote is on the continental shelf of Africa after all; it belongs to Spain only politically. Therefore, African souvenirs are appropriate for this latitude – at least the shop proprietors think so.

The Nuestra Señora de los Remedios Church has maintained its sanctified atmosphere despite the number of visitors during the past few years. The especially famous aspects of this church are the carvings and paintings on the ceilings and the reclined Jesus in a glass sarcophagus. Mass takes place on Saturdays at 5 and 7 pm and Sundays at 10 am, noon and 5 pm.

Beyond the church, one can climb the hill next to a parking area to a memorial plaque. Since 1980, it has commemorated the fact that none of the feared volcanoes has erupted for over 250 years.

Leaving the town and heading west toward El Golfo and Janubio, the road leads by the "Galería Yaiza" shortly before the edge of town. This gallery was designed by César Manrique. Various painters and sculptors exhibit in this gallery; it is open Monday to Saturday between 5 and 7 pm.

Yaiza / **Practical Information**
Accommodation →*Playa Blanca*

Restaurants
The Garden Restaurant "La Era" is on the way to El Golfo to the left of the main road. It is set back about 200 yards from the roadway. This is where the Island's newspaper staff of "Lancelot" celebrated its sixth anniversary together with some VIP's from Lanzarote. Put more precisely, Antonio Coll, the editor of this newspaper hosted 200 guests. The "La Era" is considered not only reasonably priced but also a cozy restaurant with rooms for private parties. Audio-visual shows on the island and its attraction are also part of the attraction here.

"Los Remedios" Restaurant, behind the church on the square. Ample parking is available. This restaurant also serves snacks and light meals. Take-away available.

"La Vista" Restaurant, shortly before leaving town to the west in the direction of Playa Blanca. Also located here is a souvenir shop selling items produced in North Africa and sold as Lanzarotan specialities. A stroll around this area is by all means worthwhile.

Important Addresses
Currency Exchange: Caja Insular de Ahorros, Plaza Nuestra Señora de los Remedios 14, Tel: 83 01 68.
Tourist Information/City Hall: Plaza Nuestra Señora de los Remedios, Tel: 83 01 02.
Police: Carretera Montaña del Fuego, Tel: 82 01 17; Plaza Nuestra Señora de los Remedios, Tel: 83 01 02.

Ye

Ye, the largest village in the northeastern regions of Lanzarote lies between the scenic overlook →*Mirador del Rio* and the →*Cueva de los Verdes* on the road GC 710. On the one hand, Ye is widely known for its wines sold to the right of the road when heading south and for its extensive cochineal production (→*Vegetation*), vineyards and vegetable gardens.

Youth Hostels →*Accommodation*

Those Holiday Flavours at Home

The following should prove for a flavourful evening seasoned with holiday memories.

Aguacate con gambas
(avocado with prawns)

This classical starter is the perfect beginning for a festive meal. One tip: stir some yogurt or sour cream into the mayonnaise for a lighter and more refreshing flavour.

Ingredients
2 ripe avocados
½ pound of prawns or shrimps
1 to 2 lemons

Ingredients for the sauce (Salsa rosa)
2 tablespoons mayonnaise
2 tablespoons sour cream
2 teaspoons tomato paste
2 teaspoons mustard
2 teaspoons cognac
2 teaspoons lemon juice
salt

Preparation
Cut avocados into halves and remove the pit. With a teaspoon, carefully remove the fruit and cut into small pieces. Mix with lemon juice immediately to prevent it from turning brown
Mix with cooked and peeled prawns or shrimps and place the mixture back into the avocado shell. Chill. Mix all ingredients for the sauce thoroughly and salt to taste. Pour sauce over the avocado halves before serving.

Serves 4
preparation time: 20 minutes

Also try the following more simple variation on this theme: mix the avocado pieces with canned tuna, mayonnaise and lemon juice; serve in the avocado shell as above.

Paella valenciana

Paella is the most widely known Spanish national dish. While the Valencian saffron rice originally had only fish and vegetables, it is the diverse combination of ingredients which lends this dish its character today. Pork and lamb, chicken and duck, even ham is mixed in with all types of seafood and vegetables. With some imagination there are no limits to the various creations which can be produced: this famous saffron rice is not boiled immediately but first sautéed in olive oil and then cooked in the stock from the other ingredients.

Ingredients:
2 chicken legs
1 pork cutlet
⅓ pound green beans
1 carrot
1 red bell pepper
1 medium onion
1 large tomato
1 pound mussels
½ pound octopus
4 prawns (uncooked)
1 cup rice
1 teaspoon saffron
4 tablespoons olive oil
salt
fresh ground pepper
4 lemons

Preparation
Scald and peel tomatoes, remove seeds and dice. Chop the onion and red bell pepper. Wash the mussels, octopus and prawns and slice the octopus into small pieces.
Heat 1 tablespoon olive oil in a deep frying pan and brown the octopus. Add tomato and red bell pepper as well as the prawns. Salt and pepper to taste. Simmer covered until the bell pepper is almost soft (around 30

to 45 minutes. Remove the prawns after around 10 minutes, peel and set aside.

In the meantime, boil the green beans and the carrot in saltwater. Skin the chicken legs and debone if desired. Remove any excess fat from the chicken and pork and cut into bite-sized pieces (the chicken can also be halved or left whole).

Bring 3 cups of water to a boil adding a small onion. Add mussels and steam for five minutes. Discard the shells and set the mussels aside in the broth.

In a large pan or in the same pan in which the vegetables and octopus were sautéed, add the pieces of meat and brown on all sides in 1 tablespoon olive oil; salt and pepper to taste; set aside.

Heat 1-2 tablespoons olive oil in the same pan. Sauté onion and rice. Add saffron. Cook for around 5 minutes stirring constantly. Add 2 cups of mussel broth followed by the meat and the mixture of octopus and vegetables; stir carefully. Simmer over low to medium heat an additional 20 minutes. Do not stir; only shake the pan. Shortly before the 20 minutes are up, fold in the remaining vegetables, prawns and mussels and heat. Serve with lemon wedges.

In Spain, paella is usually prepared for larger parties in a huge paella pan.

Serves 4
preparation time: 1 hour
cooking time: 35 minutes

Sangria (red wine punch)

The world renowned red wine punch with fruit pieces proves especially refreshing during the warm days of summer. Of the numerous recipes varying mainly in the types of fruits, the amount of sugar and type of brandy used. The following is our favourite.

Ingredients
1 lemon
1 orange
1 apple
1 ripe peach
around 1 cup sugar
1 bottle of light red wine
½ bottle of ice-cold soda water
a shot of brandy to taste

Preparation
Peel the lemon and orange, remove the seeds and cut into small pieces. The apple should also be peeled and quartered and then cut into bite-sized pieces as well, removing the core. Peel the peach, remove the pit and cut into small pieces.
Place the fruit pieces into a large container, sprinkle them with sugar and add the red wine. Stir well. Chill for several hours stirring occasionally. Before serving, dilute with soda water and add a shot of brandy to taste. Stir and serve over ice.

Serves 4
preparation time: 20 minutes
setting time: 3 to 4 hours